J   £2.50

*We travelled to the mountains of Portugal with a
boy, a dog and three horses and we found...*

Paradise

SANDRA CROSS

CONTENTS

ACKNOWLEDGEMENTS

A very BIG THANK YOU to my dear friend Sue Clarkson, who edited my ramblings and got them into some sort of order. She also painted the wonderful book cover portraying my home. A truly talented lady.

Also thanks to Patricia Maybourne, Denise Collin, Adam Gaisford and Andy Peters for their input and help. Beijinhos to you all.

WRITERS INFO

Sandra was born in Brighton, and lived in the Brighton area, until moving to Portugal in 1994. She started life as a shorthand typist, and has three children and four grandchildren who she loves to visit in her camper van. She has been passionate about horses since her first encounter when she was only seven years old. She still lives in her Paradise home with her husband Steve and her four dogs.

This is her first book which she thoroughly enjoyed writing; she hopes to write a sequel very soon.

This book is dedicated to all my family.

MY BOOK DESCRIPTION

After several years dreaming of a different lifestyle, we finally hit the road. Leaving our comfortable home in England, we set off with our nine year old son, our dog, and our four horses, and headed for the mountains of Portugal.

We bought a ruin, and stepped back 100 years in time. I wanted to know how life was lived without electricity, running water or machinery. What was life like without mod cons? Were people happier in those times, with very little? Our Portuguese neighbours, and our many animals have enriched our lives along the way, and all have their own story to tell.

It has been an amazing experience which I am proud to have done.

We have had some great adventures, and some tough times, but I have loved every minute of it, and I hope that you enjoy sharing our ongoing story.

CHAPTER 1

OUR SECOND BIG ADVENTURE

November 1994...The hiss of air brakes on our horsebox signalled journey's end. Steve jumped down from the truck, and after stretching his limbs, gave a little sideways leap and clicked his heels as he walked towards me, looking jubilant. "We've done it, we've arrived." I wound down the window excitedly, and he leant in to give me a kiss.

"I'm off to find Miguel," he said. I watched him as he loped up the street with his long easy stride, the afternoon sun exposed streaks of auburn in his curly black hair. Craig, our 9-year-old mini Steve, was sitting next to me; he leapt out of the car to follow after his dad. I gazed tiredly at the back of our beautiful 25 foot fairground caravan, with its chrome panels and lace curtains, which was to become our home for the next six months. Steve had towed it behind our 7.5 ton 1969 Ford D series horsebox, housing our four lovely horses. The horsebox was made of mahogany with a fibreglass roof which gave it plenty of light. I had become quite familiar with the sight of these two vehicles since we left the Spanish port of Santander, 26 hours earlier, as I struggled to stay on their tail.

Steve had driven our precious cargo of animals, towing the caravan, whilst I did my best to stay behind him in our trusty old Vauxhall Cavalier, towing a second smaller caravan. We had meandered our way slowly through Spain and Portugal, and at every town or village our convoy passed through, people in the streets had shouted and waved to us, thinking the circus was coming to town! Whilst Steve and Craig were looking for Miguel, who was a Portuguese property agent we'd met in London, I reflected on our journey.

We'd had our share of mishaps, starting before we even hit the road! We had estimated that our four horses would have to be loaded into the horsebox by 2.00am. which would give us plenty of time to drive from Brighton to Plymouth to catch the ferry at 9.00am. My favourite horse Roxy, indignant at being disturbed from his slumber, adamantly refused to go into the horsebox despite the fact that we had been practising the loading routine for weeks. It took us three hours and a vet's tranquilliser to finally persuade him! Once he was finally loaded, the other three horses; Guv, Smartie and Tawny were all a doddle, walking into their stalls in our horsebox without any fuss. We were finally on the road three hours late so Steve set a fast pace, but luck was against us; the truck seemed unsteady, but it was nothing serious, just a wheel almost falling off! By the time tools had been found and the wheel secured, we had lost another half hour.

When we arrived at the dock, we were greeted to the sight of the ferry already sailing away towards the horizon. In winter time the ferries only sailed twice a week, so we had three days to wait for the next one, and with four horses to care for, we had to get ourselves organized! After a few phone calls, we found stables near Ivybridge on the edge of Dartmoor, willing to board the horses; luckily it had a campsite opposite.

After making the horses comfortable, we settled into the caravan for the night, feeling very sorry for ourselves. It was freezing cold, we lit the wood burner in the caravan and were soon cosy. We had bought the caravan only recently from a travelling circus family; they had lived in it so it was well kitted out, with a full size cooker, a fridge and a comfortable wrap around sofa which pulled out into a large double bed, there was also a separate bedroom, and plenty of cupboard space. Above the burner was a huge cut glass mirror which added to the feeling of space; it was really quite luxurious. We were so happy when we found it for sale; we had been searching for a large roadworthy van for months and had seen some really awful ones. Large caravans are frequently used on building sites as temporary accommodation for workers and we looked at quite a few that smelt of a mixture of urine and mould! This van had obviously been loved and cared for, and because it belonged to a fairground family who moved frequently, it was in good roadworthy condition.

There was a storm forecast; the rain was already pounding onto the roof and the wind was buffeting against the windows, but we were warm and dry, our dog Toby, a black Labrador cross, was curled up in front of the fire. We should have been on our way to sunny Portugal, but on a night like this, I was happy to be on dry land.

Next morning, one of our horses, a lovely strawberry roan Arab called Tawny, was ill. He was lying down, rolling constantly on the floor of his stable and sweating profusely. We called the local vet and he diagnosed colic. He treated him and left us to keep an eye on him for the next few hours. By mid-afternoon the colic had not subsided, and the vet asked us to bring him to his practise, where he could be monitored closely. At 8pm, we had a phone call from the vet, Tawny needed surgery; we would have to take him to a specialist at Bristol Veterinary University.

We arrived at the University just before 1am. It was a huge campus, there were signs pointing in all directions, we hadn't realised that it was the main university of Bristol, the veterinary department was just one small part. It was very dark, we drove round and round, finally seeing a sign pointing down a narrow alley; it was pitch black, we came to what looked like a dead end, and were wondering what to do when a large roller door opened. Lights flooded out onto the dark lane; we were greeted by the surgeon who wasted no time in leading Tawny into a brightly lit padded cell. Bleary-eyed yawning veterinary students had been summoned from their beds by the vet to view the operation as it was a rare type of colic not often encountered. They now surrounded the poor horse as the vet pulled on elbow high gloves. Tawny was a model patient even though he was obviously in great pain. We left him in the hands of one of Britain's best vets with a 50 – 50 chance of survival.

Thankfully the operation was a success and he survived, but he would need a long convalescence, and would not be coming with us to Portugal. Tawny belonged to my sister Jenny, she had decided to give him to us only because he and Roxy had been great friends for 12 years and she didn't want to break up their friendship. Ironically, Roxy's reluctance to go into the horsebox, which caused us to miss the ferry, had saved his old friend's life. If we had sailed, and Tawny had developed colic on the boat, he could have died; now once he recovered he would be on his way back to Brighton.

Back at the campsite, Steve spent the next day buying firewood and trying to find someone to sell us some hay. Between the showers, Craig and I walked the horses out for exercise around the pretty country lanes bordering Dartmoor. We were anticipating catching the mid-week ferry and had booked a vet in case we needed help loading Roxy again. However, storms and lashing rain meant that this ferry would also sail without us, as the captain would not take animals on board in over a force 6 wind; so it was one week later that we finally arrived at the dock. The captain was still not certain about the weather conditions, the forecast was showing up to force 6, but from a southerly direction. I think this clinched it for us, because the captain said that with the wind coming from the south we would be sailing head on into it, so the boat would not be rolling too much, making it more comfortable for the horses. Finally he gave his permission for our little convoy to board the ferry, and Steve joined the queue of trucks that were already waiting. Meanwhile Craig, Toby the dog, and I drove onto the ferry in our car with the little caravan full of our worldly goods towing behind. Toby had to stay in the car, he was only allowed out for a couple of walks on the lower deck for the whole twenty-four hour duration of the journey. Luckily he had a strong bladder! From the deck, we looked down on the waiting trucks. Our truck and caravan were dwarfed by the huge juggernauts parked alongside it. I couldn't see Steve, but knew he was sitting patiently waiting to board. I had a moment of unease at the enormity of our adventure as I stood leaning over the railings, but it was too late now, we were committed.

Truck drivers on the twenty-four hour ferries are treated like kings. Whilst Craig and I were eating cardboard tasting croissants, Steve was feasting on delicious muesli with fresh and dried fruits, smothered in yoghurt. His lunchtime buffet included asparagus and artichokes, prawns and parma ham, and of course plenty of French bread. Huge bowls of fresh fruit salad and jugs of cream were laid on the tables; real coffee pots full of aromatic coffee were placed on the tables for him to help himself, whilst I sipped a muddy tasting concoction from a plastic cup.

A French steward noticed Steve smuggling food out of their dining room, and when Steve told him of his family outside the door, he threw his arms up into the air in mock horror. "Bring them in you fool, there is more than enough food here." Craig and I, teased by the wonderful smells, entered the all male dining room. We were welcomed in and couldn't believe our eyes at the sight of the buffet laid out before us; the ferry companies really did look after their truck drivers! I have never been so spoilt in my life; my plate was filled with garlic prawns, couscous salad with a variety of dressings, warm French bread and too many cheeses to choose from! There were even prawns served next morning for breakfast! For the rest of the trip, Craig, in particular, became a mascot for the truck drivers who always made sure he had the sweetest of treats, especially two drivers from the British navy who told us they were on a run to deliver parts to a ship in Lisbon. When pressed into what parts, they declined to tell us what their cargo was. It was all a bit 'hush hush'.

We had been sailing for about two hours when I asked at the information desk if I could go below deck to check on the horses. I had been told beforehand that I would be able to do this as long as I had a steward to accompany me. The steward was a young friendly French lad who spoke a bit of English. He showed an interest in seeing the horses for 5 minutes, then realising that I was going to be a while, he leaned against the horsebox, and taking out a pack of Gauloises cigarettes, lit up and waited patiently for me to feed and water the horses. On the way back up the steps onto the deck, when I explained to him that I would need to come down every two hours to check on the horses, he turned to me and in his beautiful French accent said, "Don't worry, next time, just come down by yourself, take as long as you like." I took him at his word and spent lots of time with the horses under the sea. I was feeling relaxed and happy, my horses were fine and my stomach was full; but when we landed at Santander it was a different story.

Steve had spent time before we set out, studying maps and working out the best route to take; this part of our preparations was of no interest to me. I have no sense of direction, nor can I map read. I had never driven on the right-hand side of the road before, or ever towed anything except for the short trip from Brighton to Plymouth. I coped with this by telling myself that all I had to do was follow right behind Steve. I didn't need to concern myself with anything else except keeping right on his tail. I was soon to realize what a short-sighted attitude this had been. When we left the ferry, Steve drove off first with the other trucks, and by the time we disembarked he was nowhere to be seen. I panicked...

We drove down a ramp, and more or less straight into the flow of a huge roundabout, I could see that there was nowhere that Steve could have pulled such a large rig over, it was so busy and police were keeping the traffic moving. But which way do I go? Which lane should I be in? Only Craig's cool composure kept us going. "We will keep driving until we see dad, he won't go on without us," he said calmly. I kept getting into the wrong lane. Weaving from lane to lane with a caravan in tow, and in a state of near hysteria, is no joke! The Spanish drivers were great, I met with no road rage, just tolerance and patience. I suppose living in such a busy port, they are used to crazy foreigners trying to go the wrong way around their traffic system!

Finally we saw the horsebox way ahead of us, we raced confidently (by this time I was an expert) around the roundabout. "Follow that horsebox," we cried joyfully, but the traffic lights were against us, and we lost sight of him. We drove through town, and were approaching the motorway, where I would have to make a decision on which way to go. Why, oh why, had I not studied the maps? I had left it all up to Steve, and now I was paying the price for burying my head in the sand, something that I'm very good at! We desperately hoped that Steve would wait for us as soon as he was able to pull over, when, hey presto, waiting in a lay-by, there he was. Phew.

After this I was determined to stay on his tail, but it wasn't always easy, our old Vauxhall struggled up steep inclines towing its heavy load, whilst the horsebox with its lower gearing and 6 litre engine, pulled very well up hills, and we certainly met some hills! The horsebox engine overheated as we climbed for a solid hour up the Picos Mountains. We had to make a couple of stops to let her cool down. These coastal mountains are pretty spectacular and it's fascinating how they peter out into the huge plains of Castile and Leon. We felt that we would definitely like to come back to explore this region sometime in the future, and in more clement weather...it was pouring.

The camaraderie of truck drivers is amazing. Trucks were flashing their lights and honking as they passed us on route, obviously remembering us from the ferry. We had just pulled into a layby with the rain lashing down, when a Dutch truck pulled in behind us. "Is everything all right, do you need any help," said this huge blonde handsome Dutchman, filling the doorway of our caravan. "No thanks, we are O.K. The old girl gets a bit hot going up these mountains, but she will be fine in ten minutes." Steve answered hopefully, as the steam poured out of the engine.

"O.K. I hope you've got good brakes," he said as we told him where we were heading. "Be careful going down!" He waved cheerfully and honked his horn as he passed us. The minute he pulled away, the British Navy truck pulled into the layby, it was the two guys whom we had befriended on the ferry. They both jumped down from their truck to see if we were okay, saying they were both mechanics so could help out if needed. Steve was sure it was not a problem. "It's a pin hole in the expansion tank, which only causes problems on big, long hills when the motor gets hot," he explained. "As long as we keep topping up the water and stop frequently, it should be okay, we are nearly at the top now; but thanks for the offer." They waved and set off on their mysterious journey.

We were now on a plateau that runs from the mountains above Santander right across Spain until near Guarda in Portugal. Scattered across the countryside were hundreds of very pretty little light brown ponies, with flaxen manes and tails. They seemed to be wild, as I could see no fences. At our next stop, an English truck driver pulled up; we were making tea at the time so he stopped to have one with us. He sat there, telling horror stories about trucks with brake failures going down the steep mountain range in Portugal, just after Guarda; he told of a very steep descent with multiple escape routes for vehicles suffering from brake problems. I didn't need to hear this so I went to tend to the horses, who were grateful for our regular stops. I fed them all some carrots which they munched happily, then, after saying our goodbyes to our new friend, we were on the road again. Craig swapped between us, he loved the truck but it had no cassette player. Even if it had, it would have been impossible to hear anything above the noise of the engine. He had brought some of his own cassettes, so I sometimes had the pleasure of his company. Now he was travelling with Steve in the truck, it was still raining hard, the wipers on our car had never worked so hard, as the ten combined wheels of the truck and caravan constantly threw rainwater at my windscreen. I could just make out the thick bulk of mountains through the ceaseless noise of water. I had to concentrate hard on keeping up with the truck, yet I still felt the aura and stunning beauty of the mountains. I was feeling more confident in my towing abilities and as the little caravan trundled along behind me, the rain finally ceased and the sun poked through clouds. 'The Doors' sang out on my cassette player and as I sang along with them, I began to enjoy my own private adventure.

Night fell; we were on the E80 between Salamanca and Ciudad Rodrigo, I was feeling very tired and watching out hopefully for Steve's indicators to flash on; ahead I saw lights, a garage maybe? The indicator on our caravan in front of me, flickered on and the whole rig slowed down, and we pulled into a garage/truck park at about midnight. My limbs had seized up, I almost crawled out of the car, feeling ancient! Toby the dog, leapt out full of energy and begging for a walk. Everything was quiet so I walked with him to nearby wasteland and took off his lead.

There was a rather garish pink hotel and restaurant attached to the garage, we had noticed a few of these brightly painted hotels along the E80 route. The lights were on and the smells that escaped into the night air were delicious. I wandered over to see if they were still serving, my tummy rumbling loudly. Yes - I could see truck drivers with huge plates of food and also some scantily dressed girls propped on the bar stools...a bit strange in this out of the way location! The next thing I heard was growling and snarling as a dogfight broke out. Toby, in true British 'lager lout' fashion had picked a fight with the restaurant's guard dog, which was merely doing its job. I called him and luckily he came back, wagging his tail, tongue lolling out as if nothing had happened. I took him back to the car in disgrace, and after feeding and watering the horses, we had a midnight feast at the restaurant, before crashing out exhausted, in the caravan. We had come to the conclusion that these garish hotels that were spaced out along this route were probably brothels!

We slept for a couple of hours, but trucks kept pulling in and out all through the night, their drivers chatting, and slamming doors. Needless to say, we were all a bit red eyed in the morning as we set off on the last leg of our journey.

At the Portuguese border, there was a detour in the road with a sign saying 'Trucks this way', I drove straight through, but Steve and Craig followed the arrows for trucks. I pulled up on the other side, I was in Portugal, but they were in Spain, I desperately hoped there would not be a problem; we were only 80 miles from our destination. As I sat there, imagining the worst, the horsebox with Steve and Craig both grinning from ear to ear, came rumbling past. "Whoopee, we're in Portugal," Craig shouted from the open window. I gave Toby a hug to welcome him to our new home country. Later Steve told me that he had driven around an enormous car park looking for someone to show the paperwork to, but there was not a soul in sight. We had gone to a lot of expense to make sure all the horses' documents and veterinary papers were up to date before we left Brighton, but had to go through the whole process again in Plymouth, because horses have to be checked for health within 48 hours of boarding the boat. Yet not one person on the whole trip asked to see our papers.

Now at 2 p.m. we had arrived. Eighty-five feet of truck, caravans, and car, nearly blocking the narrow cobbled street of Arganil, in Central Portugal. It had been 3 days since we had left Plymouth. Suddenly Toby jumped into the front seat, his lips curled up into a doggy smile, his tail wagging, I looked up and saw Steve, Miguel, and Craig coming towards me. "Sandra, my dear, how nice to see you, we were expecting you hours ago," said Miguel in his wonderful Latin accent. "You don't realise how slowly we travel in our little convoy," I said, as I got out of the car. Miguel was a tall, slim young man with an inexhaustible enthusiasm for his country; especially the Central Region where his family had lived for generations. He greeted me in the Portuguese way of one kiss on each cheek; this is done barely brushing the cheek, and kissing the air, very difficult to master. I have, on more than one occasion, nearly knocked the glasses off the faces of unsuspecting people with my clumsiness!

Miguel was an estate agent; we had met him originally in London, at an overseas property exhibition in early 1994. Steve and I had been dreaming of sunnier climes, and had visited the exhibition, with the idea of maybe looking for a house in France, as we had friends living in the Charente area and had enjoyed many holidays there. We were talking to a man on the stand for French properties, and telling him that we had horses and wanted a place with land, when my eye was caught by the man on the next stand, gesticulating for us to come and talk to him.

Miguel introduced himself in perfect English, and told us he specialised in properties around the area of Central Portugal. We knew nothing about Portugal, and hadn't been considering it, but he was so enthusiastic that the area was perfect for us and our horses, that we agreed to go for a holiday and have a look. And that is how our first adventure came about.

CHAPTER 2

OUR FIRST BIG ADVENTURE

May 1994...We kept in touch with Miguel, and he told us that he could book us into a brand new campsite and he had some nice properties to show us whenever we were ready. So, in April 1994 we bought a 1972 Bedford CF camper van, and in May, we took a month's holiday, and the three of us set off on our first big adventure. My two older children Paul, who was 21, and Mella, who was 17, were busy with their studies, so had stayed at home near Brighton, to look after the animals (and no doubt throw a few parties!)

We caught the ferry from Newhaven to Dieppe. When we arrived at Newhaven to board the ferry, the guy who was directing the traffic onto the boat pulled us over. He called into his radio, "I've got a camper van with a lump here, where shall I put it?" It sounded so funny we decided to call our new home 'Camper van with a lump.'

We spent about ten days in France visiting our friends Steve and Carrie and their two boys. We looked at some wonderful farms at incredibly reasonable prices, but for some reason, we both couldn't wait to get to Portugal.

We took the scenic route, wanting to get a feel for the place, you miss so much of the real essence of a country if you just stick to the motorways, and anyway our old camper van was slow, so we had nothing to gain by travelling on the faster roads.

The van had a roof, which was hinged on one side. When stationary, we lifted the roof to give us more height; there was also a little pull out bed for Craig in the roof space. The weight of the roof was supported by two gas filled pistons (the same as on the tail gates of hatchbacks and estate cars). One windy night, I heard a little voice saying, "Mum, the roof has fallen on me." In my half-conscious sleepy state, I muttered "Be quiet and go to sleep."

"But mum, I can't move." Turning over, warm and comfortable, and thinking that he was dreaming, I again urged him to go to sleep.

"Dad, will you believe me, the roof has fallen on me." came the miserable sounding reply. Grumpily Steve reached for the torch, and got up to have a look. There was our poor son, trapped like a Breville sandwich between the bed and the roof! The pistons had been forced down by the strong wind. Luckily he was only a skinny little 8 year old, but he never trusted the pistons again, and always had two sticks of wood wedged between the bed and the roof, to act as a back-up system.

The roads in Portugal were, and in some places still are, terrible! Our little camper van had back opening doors, and driving through England, France and Spain, we had no problems, but when we hit Portugal and the potholes, the back doors would fly open without any warning every time the van bounced over a hole or a bump in the road. Anything that was not tied down would be strewn over the road behind us. On two or three occasions, we had to stop, and run back to retrieve a bag of bread rolls or a pair of shoes, that had been bounced out as the van lurched over another pothole, and the door flew open!

Apart from the potholes, I loved everything about Portugal; the contrasts of mountains and valleys, so different from the rolling countryside back home. I felt like I had stepped back 100 years, to a time before great machines made it unfeasible to keep hedgerows, when you could look down on land as a patchwork of small fields rotating different crops. Below me as we drove along the sides of valleys, I could see maize growing, bordered by grapevines, and olive orchards, with sheep grazing beneath their canopy. An ox stood patiently hitched to his cart as his owner worked in the fields. People were tending their fields, not leaving it to pesticide sprays. There was a feeling of life.

True to his word, Miguel directed us to a little town called Góis, that nestled in a deep narrow valley, surrounded by heather clad mountains. The river Ceira flowed through the middle of the town, and we walked along the river bank, and through a park of ancient trees that gave spectacular late Autumn colour. A set of stone steps led up to a new campsite. Roger and Peggy were the new proprietors; they were a

Belgian couple, who had been to Portugal on holidays and decided to make a life change, just as we wanted to do. Their original idea was to buy some land and build a campsite, it was a total coincidence that Góis council had spent seven years building a campsite above the town, and had just put it out to tender when Roger and Peggy happened to be passing through town in their camper van, and met Miguel. He persuaded them to place a bid for the tender which they won. They were actually the only people to apply for the contract. Roger and Peggy were a gregarious, friendly couple starting out on a new adventure of their own.

The campsite was not officially open yet but they were happy for us to stay with them for a week while Miguel took us out every day to see a variety of properties; we fell in love with one of them. It was about five acres of flat fertile land with river frontage, perfect for horses. Across a country lane, was another plot with planning permission for a house, Steve had often promised me that one day he would build me a house; here was his chance!

The owners gave us a rough price that was just about within our pockets; the problem was twelve different factions of the family owned it, which was common in Portugal. A father would split his land up into however many pieces he had children, then in turn, a child who had been left one fifth of his father's land, then had 3 children himself and split that fifth up into thirds, and so on and so on. It could end up with one person owning two square metres of land, and no paper work! It was crazy, and very frustrating for someone trying to buy. This law has since been changed, it is much more difficult to split land these days.

Miguel had told us that this was the most beautiful region of Portugal, especially around the Góis area, but you can't trust everything a real estate agent says. We wanted to see more of Portugal, and give the family who wanted to sell a week or so to think about things and try to sort out some paperwork. We packed up our camper and headed on down to the coast.

We drove through a forest between the coast and Marinha Grande. Pine trees had been grown there since the 13th century to help keep the sand dunes at bay, and also to grow wood for the maritime industry. The scent of the old pine trees is something I remember to this day, but sadly over 80% of this wonderful forest, that spread over 100 square kilometres was destroyed by fire in 2017. We ate a late picnic lunch among the pines then headed on towards the coast.

The wild western Atlantic coast is breathtakingly beautiful; and it has some of the most dramatic coastline, with ancient dunes and jagged cliffs. I dreamed about how wonderful it would be to gallop on Roxy along the expansive sandy beaches. We travelled through Sao Pedro De Moel, which was a really pretty, well-kept seaside town and was probably a popular holiday resort for richer Portuguese people. On a rocky outcrop stood a lighthouse called Penedo da Saudade; further along the coast we turned onto a sandy track which led to what I can only describe as 'tent city'. It was totally deserted except for a few hungry dogs, yet some of the tents looked quite nice; we surmised that maybe it was a weekend holiday destination. It looked a perfect place to stay for the night, the sun was still quite warm in the late afternoon, so we parked under a pine tree for shade. We could hear the Atlantic waves crashing onto the shore, so we walked through the dunes to take a look. Steve and Craig actually did some body surfing in the freezing water; I was content to just paddle! Later Steve lit our little barbecue and cooked some chops, the tantalising smell attracted a poor little hungry dog. I couldn't enjoy my meal under his starving gaze, so I emptied half my food onto an old tin plate that we had found and tried to approach him; he slunk off into the vegetation so I put the plate down for him and later I noticed him nervously returning to eat his chop.

We all slept well, the coastal breeze whispered through the pines, lulling us to sleep. Next morning our windscreen was splashed with pine resin which had leaked from the tree that we had unwittingly parked under, hence we spent the next half hour with washing up liquid and scrapers, trying to clean the windscreen! Finally after much scrubbing, the windscreen was still smudged but Steve could see through it, so we set off to explore another beach. At Praia da Polvoeiro we saw a beautiful 3 foot long, green lizard slithering down a sand dune towards us, it scuttled swiftly away almost running over our feet in its panic. Polvoeiro is an extensive bay surrounded by cliffs and forests. We went for a long walk along the sand, the sea was calm, we had been told it was easy to spot octopus in the clear rocky waters, but we were out of luck. We did spot dolphins though, and as we ate our delicious seafood lunch, we told our waiter of our sightings. He said it was quite common to see them, and told us a wonderful legend of a poet called Arion who was flung overboard by pirates after he sang his Swan song. Legend has it that he was rescued by a dolphin who heard his melodious voice and brought him safely back to shore.

Next morning we drove to Nazaré, there had obviously been a good sardine catch earlier that morning, and many women were busy slicing sardines in half down the centre, sprinkling them with salt and drying them on racks in the sunshine. There were hundreds of these racks and thousands of fish. We had never seen anyone eating them or been offered them in a restaurant, so we assumed it was just for local consumption. Our eyes were drawn further along the beach to two teams of six oxen standing patiently on the sandy shore. A group of men were folding nets into a beautifully painted boat with a very high prow. As we walked closer, I could see an eye painted on the prow. The ladies salting the sardines tried to explain the meaning of the eye. I understood it as being the eye to see either storms or shoals of fish! I asked if the boat was going out again and they all nodded in unison. We decided to sit on the beach and watch. Half an hour later, the boat was pushed down into the surf, a group of men all jumped into the boat, grabbing a long oar each. They skillfully steered the boat directly into the crashing surf; a really big breaker almost sent the boat up vertical, but the men held their positions and dug into the surf with the oars until they were through to the calmer waves. They started up an outboard motor and went about a kilometre out to sea, they then changed direction and travelled about the same distance parallel to the shore, all the time dropping their nets. A rope which remained on shore was dragged by the boat, it was threaded through a sleeve at the top end of the nets and now sat on the surface of the sea as the weighted nets sunk below. The sailors then turned towards the beach and sailed back into the surf, still holding the other end of the rope. The rope was thrown to the waiting men standing on the shore, with their oxen team; the other end of rope that had been left on the shore was harnessed to a second team of oxen further along the beach. The two teams gradually moved closer together as the net came closer in, so that the net was like a huge balloon. It took about two hours to slowly haul in the nets (hopefully) full of fish. The fish were then hauled flapping and squirming onto the beach and were auctioned off straight away to waiting restaurateurs and to the public looking for their fish supper. The remainder were taken to the nearby market. I noticed an impoverished family picking up the smaller fish and putting them into a bag, nobody shouted at them or asked them for money. Craig was very upset by the poor fish gasping on the shore, he picked up some of the bigger fish and was gently putting them back in the sea. I expected someone to scold him, but nobody did, everyone was in high spirits and they just smiled at him as he took another flailing fish back to the sea. The seagulls were circling and crying excitedly for their tit bits, which they would surely get once the crowd moved on. There was plenty for everyone.

The sun was setting on a low tide, the three of us strolled along the now almost deserted beach. The sky was shot through with purples, pinks, and crimsons, which on the gleaming wet sand, created a mirror image. The effect was so mesmerizing that we forgot to take photos until it was so dark that we were just silhouettes in the background.

It had been another extraordinary day. I don't even know if the boats still operate in the same way, it's a dangerous way to make a living but I loved watching my little boy rescuing a few lucky fish.

We noticed a funicular railway at the bottom of the biggest cliff. Craig was eager to ride on it, so we promised him we would come back next morning and see what was up on top of the cliff. We all slept well that night in our little camper van with a lump! Next morning we all boarded the funicular; it was very exciting to have a seagulls eye view of the cliffs and the coast way below us. When we reached the top, we were in a large square dominated by a beautiful ornate church from the 18th century. All around the square, lots of older ladies were garishly dressed in short skirts with layers of petticoats, selling local produce. They looked really bizarre; folklore has it that the fisherwomen awaiting their husbands return on the fishing boats, wore seven petticoats to help keep them warm. I can think of warmer materials than net and lace, These ladies were dressed for the tourists, I was sure. There was even an old beggar woman sitting on the steps of the church with her little pot of coins, flaunting her petticoats. We had an early delicious outdoor sardine lunch in the square, before setting off on our next adventure which was a short drive to Foz do Arelho, a beautiful inlet that feeds the lagoon of Óbidos. It has become one of our favourite beaches and we have since returned many times. Steve tried his hand at catching us some dinner and caught a fish which he was going to throw back because it wasn't very big but it had a deadly weapon - a sting! It really hurt him, a nearby fisherman saw and came over to warn us that it was dangerous, he suggested Steve should see a doctor. Shortly afterwards, Steve's hand became swollen and he felt a bit woozy so we decided to find a pharmacy. The pharmacist wasn't available until 4pm, so we had to wait with the fish still wrapped up in paper. Finally the pharmacist arrived and Steve put the fish onto the counter. There was a mad few minutes trying to describe in a foreign language, what had happened, before the chemist disappeared into his back room. When he re-emerged it was with a large tin of Waspeze. By now Steve's hand felt tingly like the sensation of an anaesthetic wearing off. The woozy feeling had subsided and he didn't want a large tin of Waspeze; so he just walked out and left the fish on the counter for the startled chemist to deal with!

A little way inland was the town of Óbidos, which had a really medieval feel, with narrow cobbled streets, and traditional blue painted cottages. The town was overlooked by an imposing medieval castle. We all walked a little way around the top of a wall which surrounded the castle, and also the whole town. The views were outstanding, but it is not a walk for the faint of heart; there were no safety barriers and it was a long way down! We had coffee and a pastry in a tiny cafe on the main street. Steve had to bow his head to get under the beam of the doorway but it was cool and dimly lit inside which gave us relief from the hot sunshine for a bit. We stayed at a campsite just outside Óbidos, and later we sat with a beer watching yet another sunset kindle the sky.

We moved on to Peniche, which is a great surfing town, Steve and Craig were very keen to get back into the waves so we booked into a campsite on the cliffs, for two nights. Craig caught some great little waves on his foam bodyboard, Steve made friends with a couple of Australian surfers who offered to lend him a board and when the waves got bigger, he had a great time too, surfing some nice waves near the harbour wall. I was happy to catch up on some sunbathing. Next day we went around to the south side of Peniche to a beach called Supertubes, which is where the serious surfers go, but unfortunately at that time the sea was glassy calm, and not a surfer in sight. One thing we hadn't counted on was that there were two sardine canning factories near the campsite, and when the wind blew in the wrong direction...'Phew', the smell!

This was as far south as we wanted to go on our trip, but we wanted to see the monastery of Alcobaça so we headed inland. Alcobaça, which has a Gothic monastery dating back to the 12th century, is a very beautiful city. The monastery with its high walls of dark stone had a rather oppressive feel, but on this warm day, it was wonderfully cool inside and had an almost unearthly aura. The kitchen of the monastery was built and covered with tiles in the mid-18th century. The central chimney is enormous, supported by eight iron columns. Water and fresh fish were diverted from the river to the kitchen basin through a specially built canal, so that the monks always had access to fresh fish. To enter the dining room, you had to be able to walk through a rather thin doorway. If you were not able to get through the door, then you couldn't eat until you had slimmed down. Now there's an idea for a new diet!

We saw many beautiful azulejos on our travels. Some, the size of a normal wall picture, were popular in cafes and restaurants, but others took up the whole wall of a building; these glazed ceramic, hand painted tiles often depicted scenes from Portuguese history. Many portrayed the great explorers who sailed the world on magnificent old wooden sailing ships, the painter managing to capture on tiles the perilous seas and brave sailors. Another popular subject to be painted on tile was horses; in particular the wonderful Lusitano horse, featured in many battle scenes and the mount of princes and kings throughout the ages. I wondered if I would ever own a Lusitano.....

That evening we had dinner at a little restaurant within the old square under the formidable walls of the monastery. In the evenings it was lit up giving it a softer, enchanted feel. We tried the popular Alentejo dish 'Carne de Porco à Alentejana,' which is diced pork, served with clams in a rich tomato sauce, and tiny diced fried potatoes -delicious! Next morning we sadly left Alcobaça and the coast, and started the long drive back to the mountains. My whole family are of coastal descent going way back to my great grandfather who was first coxswain of the Selsey Bill lifeboat in 1861. He was presented with a silver medal for long and valuable life saving service, being involved in the rescue of at least seven ships and saving many lives. I never met him but my grandmother told me many stories from her childhood of her and her mother, helping to bring injured or exhausted sailors to shore, and offering them blankets and hot drinks. I was born in Brighton and had lived on the south coast for my whole life; I must admit that I was a little sceptical of not living near the sea, yet the mountains were so beautiful, and would be much better for keeping and riding horses. If we wanted to offer horse riding holidays, then I felt that the mountains offered more diversity.

We were all keen to know if Miguel had managed to sort out any paperwork on our little patch of paradise in the mountains. Also we had to start the long drive home to Brighton; back to reality.

We drove back up to Góis to have a last meeting with Miguel and the owners of the land we wanted to buy, but you cannot hurry the Portuguese, nothing had happened in our absence. We would have to return home and leave the negotiations in Miguel's hands. We were absolutely sure that this green heart of Portugal was where we wanted to live. After saying our goodbyes to Roger and Peggy, we set off in the early evening, Steve likes to drive at night and once he gets behind the wheel he is hard to stop. We reached the Spanish border at about midnight. Craig had already crashed out on the double bed in the back of the van, I was falling asleep in my seat, so although I knew it was taboo, I crept back and snuggled up next to him. Steve drove on into the night.

Next morning, he was fast asleep, so Craig and I went for a walk to give him some more sleep time. He had parked up in a lovely little spot on a wide grass verge next to a river. As we walked along the grassy riverbank, Craig shouted out in excitement; "Look, it's full of turtles!" We counted thirty in one spot, but when they saw or heard us, they all dived in unison to the far bank, surfacing again where they had more vegetation to hide under. We called it 'Turtle Creek' and have stopped there a few more times over the years, but have never seen the turtles again. Steve had made coffee by the time we returned, he told us we were near Burgos and had a long drive ahead of us up to the Charante area where our friends Steve and Carrie lived. They were always great company, and we spent a very pleasant couple of days there, before driving up to catch the ferry. As we were leaving their house to drive to the port, Carrie said, "You have seven hours to make it to the ferry."

"No," said Steve, "we have 8 hours." Then it dawned on us that we had forgotten to change our watches. Portugal has the same time as England, but Spain and France are one hour different. We zoomed off as fast as our little van would go! Normally, 'Camper van with a Lump' liked to drive at about 50 mph but Steve was pushing her to drive up to 65 mph for most of the journey. We made it by the skin of our teeth.

We put our house on the market, thinking it could take time to sell, but as fate would have it, we found a buyer straight away. We then had a manic two months of buying two caravans, buying the horse truck, selling all our furniture, and taking Portuguese lessons from a lady who advertised in our local free paper. We didn't realise that she was Brazilian, and although a lot of the words are similar, the accent is totally different; the lessons did us no good at all! We sold our taxi business, and were ready to go. One night, we had a phone call from Miguel. The Portuguese family couldn't agree about selling the property, and the price they were now asking was beyond us anyway. We were devastated, but Miguel in his normal enthusiastic and chirpy way said "Come anyway, I'll sort something out for you and the horses temporarily." We must have taken leave of our senses, but that's exactly what we did!

CHAPTER 3

LIFE AT THE MONASTERY

November 1994...Five months later, we were all standing with Miguel, on the pavement next to the horse box in Arganil. My beautiful horses were stamping their feet and getting impatient. We were keen to find out what Miguel had in store for us. "Would you like some refreshments?" asked Miguel; "There's a café over the road."

"Yes, that would be wonderful," I answered, "But I'm worried about the horses, they need to stretch their legs." I glanced at the horsebox, swaying slightly to the rhythm of the restless stamping of twelve hooves. "Okay just a quick one," said Miguel " I can tell you about the plans I have made for you." We all walked across the narrow, cobbled street, and sat drinking coffee in the warm November sunshine, whilst Miguel told us his plans.

"About 3 kilometres from here in a little village called Folques, there is an old monastery which is now run as an agricultural college. They have plans to build a riding school, and are keen to have talks with you, would you be interested?" Our dream had been to set up a riding holiday business, leading people on horseback up into the mountains, picnicking along the way. A riding school sounded rather boring by comparison, but at the moment, we had three restless horses, no home, or land. "They have a field set aside for your horses," said Miguel, seeing our apprehensive faces.

For me that clinched it! I looked at Steve; "Yes, we are interested," he said, he had already read my mind. "Good, I'll just go and get my car, then you follow after me." Miguel went to pay for the coffees, as Steve and I walked slowly across the road. "It's a start," said Steve, ever the optimist. "Let's keep an open mind." I smiled at him, but inside I had doubts. The horsebox was still swaying, "Nearly there, boys," I called to the horses, as we climbed into the vehicles, and the engines fired up for the last leg of our long journey.

We were now travelling along a narrow winding lane, with terrible potholes, Steve drove very carefully, ever aware of the three tired horses trying to keep their balance in the back, and as we edged our way through a narrow, walled village, Steve and Craig had to pull in the mirrors on the truck to get through.

After they had successfully passed, I followed in the Cavalier, towing my own little caravan, and noticed different colour car body paints on the walls, where some drivers hadn't been so lucky! We were travelling so slowly Miguel had to keep stopping and waiting for us. I was trying to take everything in, the valley was very steep and forested, nowhere suitable for grazing a horse, but as we manoeuvred around a sharp bend in the lane, the scene that unfolded before me was like something out of an Alpine holiday brochure. Towering escarpments surrounded neat green pastures, grazed by flocks of sheep. I was so enthralled that I nearly crashed into the back of the caravan that Steve was towing, as it suddenly pulled up.

There was a banging of doors as we all jumped out. The vehicles in front of me had been blocking my view, but now as I joined the others at the front of the horsebox I could see a beautiful old building, with a huge cobbled courtyard. Through an old stone archway, I could see a fountain spurting water. On each side of the road leading to an old church, were orchards containing scores of different types of fruit and nut trees.

"Well what do you think?" asked Miguel, Steve put his arm around me, "Impressive" he exclaimed.

"It's beautiful," I voiced, gazing at 10 acres of flat green fields.

"This is the land of the agricultural college, and they are happy to lend it to you for a while," he said, splaying his arm around 180 degrees, for us to take in the wonderful views.

Over our shoulder, he waved, "Hilario, Boa Tarde." (Good afternoon.) We all turned to see a short moustached middle-aged man, walking towards us. Miguel introduced us; Hilario was the person in charge of the day-to-day running of the college. Miguel had an animated conversation with him, which included lots of pointing and arm waving, before turning to us to translate.

"You can park the caravan around the back, close to the administration block."

"OK, that's fine, but at the moment, I'm more worried about getting the horses out." I said anxiously. After more animated conversation, Miguel turned back to us. "Hilario says you can have that field over there," pointing to a rock strewn small field. "Oh" we said. Hilario must have seen our despondent faces, and asked Miguel if everything was all right. "Yes, yes," Miguel assured him, "everything is fine". It wasn't fine, but we were not in a position to argue, we had to get the horses out.

Steve unhitched the two-ton caravan, and jumped back into the truck to move it forward enough to lower the ramp. The horses had really had enough, they were kicking and stamping impatiently, the box was rolling from side to side. Miguel and Hilario, stood watching; I think they were interested to see what was going to come out; I'm not sure what they expected, but they certainly looked apprehensive!

We lowered the ramp, and I led Guv down, his head was held high, nostrils flared, he was a beautiful bright bay ex-racehorse 16.2 hands high. Standing on top of the horsebox ramp he looked huge. Hilario who had never seen an English thoroughbred before, looked impressed, Miguel nodded approvingly. Guv surveyed his new home; all the horses had worn leg bandages, and a light rug, to protect them from knocks on the journey. Steve held Guv, whilst I took off his travelling gear. Next I led out Smartie, my pretty grey Arab; he pranced lightly down the ramp, his intelligent head taking everything in. Miguel helped hold Smartie, while I took off his leg bandages and rug, then we led the two horses into the small field, and took off their head collars.

They both tossed their heads, and bucked before galloping off to the far corner, and simultaneously crumpling to the ground to roll, in sheer pleasure of being free.

We had to be quick now, it sounded as though Roxy was destroying the box! He didn't appreciate being left until last, but we had a problem: Roxy was a bully and the other two horses were afraid of him. In England, we got around this problem by erecting an electric fence across the field, so that he had his own space, but could still be close to the others, whilst they could feel safe and relaxed.

Now we had no time to unpack our electric fence system and erect it, Roxy was demanding attention! We made the decision to let him in with the others; we would erect the electric fence later. Steve led him out with difficulty; Roxy, my bay Welsh Cob, was very strong and bossy. He came crashing down the ramp, his hairy big feet sounding more like an elephant than a horse. Miguel and Hilario took several steps back; it was a struggle to get his travelling rug off, Steve could barely hold on to him as he circled around trying to rear up in a bid for freedom. Finally he was free, and he galloped off spraying us all with kicked up soil.

The other two horses had settled down and were grazing peacefully, they looked up as Roxy thundered towards them, and they made a joint decision…run! These fields were meant to contain sheep, the fencing was low, and of no obstacle to two frightened horses, they leapt the fence easily, with Roxy on their heels. They galloped on over a low ridge and disappeared from sight.

Steve, Craig and I scrambled through the fencing and ran across the field; breathlessly we reached the ridge. I couldn't believe my eyes, instead of the carnage I had expected, all three horses were standing close together, doing what they did best, eating! My fears about bullyboy Roxy were unfounded, he hadn't been chasing them, he had merely wanted to catch up with them. Guv and Smartie seemed a little nervous of their old enemy, but from that day onwards, the three shared a field, and although Roxy was definitely the boss, he showed them none of his former aggression. The only answer I can find for this change of character was that after being locked up in stressful conditions for over 60 hours, he had established a bond, a need, for the other two horses.

Miguel and Hilario strolled up behind us; after a short conversation with Hilario, Miguel turned to us. "Hilario says you might as well have this field seeing as the horses are already in it. There is a gate at the other end near the administration block where you will be parking your caravan, so access will be better for you." We were pleased with this change, because it was a much nicer field - although stony, it had better grass. and was about four times the size, very long and narrow with beautifully kept olive trees down one side. We left the horses grazing in the late afternoon sun.

Steve re-hitched the caravan, and manoeuvred it into its final location. Miguel left us with the promise to return tomorrow, bringing an extension lead, so we could plug into the college's electricity, and to discuss our future. We had sold nearly all of our furniture in England, we knew we couldn't bring it with us; we had each decided on one item that we wanted to keep. Steve had chosen his mountain bike, I loved my antique pine table, and Craig kept his old school desk which we had bought him many years before at an auction. It was a double desk with two lift up lids, two inkwells, and grooved pencil rests. The graffiti scratched wood told us Baz wos ere 1972, I luv the Beatles 1967, and of the undying love of Neil and Suzie 1968. I wonder where they are now?

These items would have to live outside for now, there was no room for them and us in the caravan. We had bought a flat pack wooden sofa with us, Steve erected it while I searched for tea bags, milk and cups; there was only one thing on my mind now, a nice cup of tea! We collapsed, exhausted, onto the newly made sofa, and enjoyed our first cup of English tea in Portugal.

We sat for an hour or so as the sun went down; a mist drifted lazily along the valley, the outline of the surrounding hills etched out against the darkening sky. It was so still; I could hear the horses grazing nearby. We opened a bottle of wine, and drank a toast to our new life, surrounded by the lush green vegetation, enveloped by the warm star-studded night - had we discovered paradise?

The next morning I woke up to the sun streaming through the caravan bedroom window; I pulled up the Venetian blinds. Roxy was standing with his head over the gate waiting for his breakfast, but he would have to wait, I had no intention of getting out of bed yet. Living in the caravan was a great novelty for Craig; he volunteered to make us tea and toast in bed; what luxury! I lay there watching the horses from my bed, Guv and Smartie stood close together, their tails swishing gently. Roxy was alert, his ears pricked forward, he could hear our voices and see movement inside the caravan; he looked so lovely standing there.

The first time I had seen him 12 years ago, he was just 6 months old. I had seen an advert in the local paper: 'Welsh cob foal for sale'. Horses were often offered for sale in the paper, it was not uncommon, yet I kept returning to this advert, and re-reading it. Steve and I had only been together for a short while; I had my work cut out with two young children, a job and a pending divorce. "I have no room in my life for a horse" I said out loud, as I went to answer the ringing phone. It was my sister Jenny. "Have you seen the advert for the Welsh foal in the paper," she exclaimed.

"Yes Jenny, but it's not the right time for me to take on a young foal, and anyway, I have your lovely Tawny to ride whenever I like, I don't need any more responsibilities at the moment."

"Oh, but he sounds so sweet" she cried plaintively.

"No Jenny! I've got to go, I'll speak to you later.... Bye."

Steve, who had been out working, came inside and picked up the newspaper. After a few minutes, he said "Have you seen this advert for a Welsh cob foal, isn't that your favourite breed?" Fate was obviously determined to get her way!

"OK," I said, "let's go and see him"

We arranged to meet the owner at 3.00pm the following day, but arrived early.

"Oh, look at him, he's gorgeous" squealed Jenny, already halfway through the fence. I followed her through, and we approached the cute little furry foal.

"Hello little babe," I said, walking slowly forward, holding out my hand to him. To our horror, the cute little furry thing laid back his ears and galloped straight towards us. He took a chunk out of my jacket, then turned like lightening and kicked my sister. Scrambling our wits together, we made a hasty exit back through the fence.

A little while later, the owner, who introduced herself as Julia, arrived. She didn't know that we had already acquainted ourselves with the monster, but it was clear by her body language that she was scared stiff of him. She grabbed some hay, ran for the stable, with the monster in hot pursuit, threw in the hay, and slammed the door shut. We all leaned over the door, watching him eat, as she told us her tale.

Her friend had bought a horse in London, and had rented a trailer to go and pick it up. She thought it would be a nice day out to accompany her friend on the journey, so the two girls set off together. Whilst they were waiting for her friend's horse to be loaded in the trailer, they went to stroke a mare and foal standing in a stable nearby. The farmer asked if they wanted to buy the foal; she knew nothing about horses, but what trouble could such a sweet little thing cause? He enchanted her; she could just keep him as a pet.

They agreed on a price and he was loaded into the trailer along with the other horse. The trouble started almost immediately; he neighed continually all the way home. By the time he was unloaded he was very distressed and sweating badly. He was obviously missing his mum, but in time he settled in with the other horse. After a few months, her friend moved away, taking the horse with her, and that was when the trouble really started. He had become uncontrollable and aggressive, she realised what a big mistake she had made.

The vet was called for routine injections, and aged him at about 6 months. By now she had owned him for 3 months, which would have made him only 3 months old when he left his mother.

"That's much too young," I said. No wonder he has a chip on his shoulder, poor little chap." Even so, I had been put off by our encounter in the field, so we told the girl we would 'let her know'.

I thought about him all night, there was something special about him; he looked identical to my first pony, whom I had loved dearly, he had been a monster too! The next morning Steve went down on one knee, and asked me to marry him. I was flabbergasted, but accepted happily.

"What would you prefer, the foal or an engagement ring?" he asked.

"The foal," I said without hesitation, "I never wear rings; you know that."

I was brought back from my daydream by a car pulling up. "It's Miguel," called Steve, who was already up and dressed. He stepped outside to welcome him, I guzzled down the remains of my tea, and jumped out of bed, I just had time to dress, wash, and run a brush through my hair, before Miguel stepped into the caravan. "Good morning Sandra, is the coffee pot on yet?" Just at that moment, there was a long 'Hooot'... "Ah the bread van," said Miguel "right on cue, let's go and choose some cakes to go with coffee."

We all strolled down to the bread van, Craig ran ahead excitedly, by the time we reached the van, a queue had already formed. It must have been the college staff's coffee break too. Craig jumped up and down, trying to see what goodies were inside, some kindly ladies ushered him to the front. The aroma of fresh bread and cakes percolated through the cool morning air, everything was sold by the kilo, even biscuits, which were sold loose, and looked home made. We stocked up on a few items, and bought half a kilo of pasteis de nata - lovely little Portuguese pastries filled with a creamy custard and flavoured with lemon zest then blasted in a hot oven until almost burnt on top...yummy with a cup of hot black coffee. We also bought still warm soft bread rolls called paposecas which roughly translates as dry dough; or dry chat! And how could we resist the local goat's cheese; we were going to have a feast.

We sat outside on our new sofa, eating cakes and drinking coffee; the sunshine was glorious, even though it was only ten o'clock in the morning. The weather in England had been typical for November, rain and wind, now it felt as if we had stepped back into summertime.

We had an appointment to see Hilario at ten thirty, so Craig and I went to prepare breakfast for the horses, who had given up waiting and had wandered off to graze. But on hearing the familiar sounds of grain falling into buckets, their ears pricked up, and they were waiting eagerly at the gate for us. As we walked to check the water trough, we noticed a little man limping towards us, "Bom dia, como esta?" (Good morning, how are you?) "Estou bem obrigada" I answered, (I am well thank you.) Basic pleasantries were about as far as my understanding of the language went. This little man, who couldn't have been more than about 4ft 9in tall, didn't know that, he was chattering away enthusiastically, pointing to the horses. I took a wild guess "Queres ver os cavalos?" (Would you like to see the horses?) "Sim,sim, Senhora" he said nodding his head and hobbling along behind us. He introduced himself as Pedro; I found it impossible to put an age to him, he didn't actually look that old, but his face was very weather beaten; he could have been any age between 40 and 65 years.

After stroking and admiring the horses, he beckoned us to follow him into the next field, which was hidden from view by bushes. There were sheep grazing contentedly, but with one whistle from the little man, they came trotting over, crowding around us. Craig was enthralled; he had never been up close to a sheep before yet now he was surrounded by about twenty, their little noses snuffling into his clothing, obviously looking for a treat. The little shepherd brought some grain from his pocket, and tipped it into Craig's hand. The biggest sheep, whose name was Joaninha, (Ladybird) nibbled the grain from his hand. "It tickles," laughed Craig. The shepherd told us all their names, how could he remember them all? They all looked the same to me!

Miguel and Steve were walking towards us, Toby came bounding up, his long pink tongue lolling out, he had been off in the woods, checking out his new territory; luckily he was well trained around sheep, and stood quietly beside us. "Bom dia Pedro," greeted Miguel, slapping the little man on the back. "Sandra, we must be going, Hilarious is waiting for us," said Miguel chuckling at his little joke. (to this day we still think of Hilario as Hilarious!) "Yes OK," I answered, " Pedro was just introducing us to his sheep." Pedro was having an animated conversation with Steve, probably about sheep; Steve could not understand him, which frustrated Pedro, so he stepped forward, as close to Steve as he could get, and shouted up at him at the top of his voice. Obviously, Steve would now understand him! It could well have been

Pedro's first encounter with a foreigner, or maybe he thought Steve was hard of hearing.

Luckily, Miguel came to the rescue. "He says your horses are very beautiful, but too big, he prefers his sheep." Steve smiled down at him. I think Pedro thought that if he stood really close and shouted at the top of his voice, we understood him. Over the next few weeks, we humored him into thinking this was true.

Hilario told us, with Miguel's help, that the council was funding a riding school. Building would start next week, There would be six stables, a hay barn, an office, and bathroom, plus a sand school. It all sounded ideal, and at the time we were happy to accept. Everyone seemed so friendly; Craig had already made a friend, a boy called Jorge. He was the son of one of the workers and about two years older than him.

Within a week, Craig was waiting eagerly for him to come home from school every day to play. Jorge taught Craig Portuguese words, and Craig taught him English; it's amazing how quickly children pick up new languages, I'm afraid the same couldn't be said for me! One evening a couple of older boys came with Jorge to visit. They introduced themselves in good English as Nuno and Carlos. Apparently, they learned their English from watching American films. They were very keen to meet the horses and said they would love to learn to ride but had no money. I had a light bulb moment...they wanted to ride and I wanted to learn to speak Portuguese. There was a simple solution to this quandary; we did a deal with them, they teach us Portuguese, and I would teach them to ride.

We started that evening and within a few days the boys had picked up walking and trotting, stopping and starting, and were keen to get off the lunge rope and out into the countryside; they knew a lot of the local tracks, so it was great for me to go out riding with them and not get lost! It was a stunning area; I didn't recognise a lot of the trees as we rode up a steep spiral hill which led up to an old chapel, where we had magnificent views over the whole of Arganil. The spiral hill was lined with very old trees with glossy dark green leaves, bright red fruit and white blossom with a tiny yellow centre.

"What are these trees called?" I asked the boys. "I don't recognise them at all, it's very rare to see a tree with fruit and blossom at the same time."

"They are called Medronho trees" called Carlos who was riding Smartie at the back of the group. He trotted up beside me so that I could hear him clearly and he told me the story of his grandfather who used to pick the berries by hand, and brewed a very strong alcohol from them. Every small village owned an alambique - which is a 'still' in English. Carlos didn't think many people made their own Medronho any more, in fact, he thought it might be illegal to make it without a licence. But it was an old Portuguese speciality and Carlos knew that some of his older relations still secretly made it. I reached up and picked one of the very pretty bright red gems which were about the size of cherry.

"Are they edible?" I asked him. "Yes, they won't hurt you, but they are not as nice as they look." Carlos wrinkled his face as I put the berry into my mouth. The texture was soft and dry, the flavour was very mild, not unpleasant but not worth risking climbing the tree to collect them. I have since learned that we can grow them in England, usually in pots and we call them the Strawberry tree.

Sometimes Craig and Jorge came with us on our rides, which meant that the four boys had to take turns in riding Guv and Smartie, but on this day I was riding with just the two older boys. There was a nice uphill narrow track coming up, I thought it looked good for a canter and because it was narrow, the horses would have to stay one behind the other and would not be tempted to race. "Would you like a canter" I called back to the boys, they were very enthusiastic, it would be their first canter but I was sure they were good enough. The three horses picked up on the excitement and as I clicked my tongue 'click click' they all set off a bit too fast; but the boys loved it, they were whooping like cowboys!

I looked forward to exploring further afield, the boys were good fun and very curious to learn about British culture. In return they really did try to teach us Portuguese but oh, my memory is so bad, I found it very hard to learn. Steve wasn't much better, but he was more outgoing than me, so whenever we went shopping or had to try to speak Portuguese, it was always him that spoke; he got more confident as I got less. Young Jorge was a natural around the horses, he was also very greedy, and had a habit of coming into the caravan and helping himself to anything edible he could find. One day Craig was making himself a Marmite roll, you could not buy Marmite in Portugal, so Jorge assuming it was chocolate, stuck his finger into the pot, and the equivalent of about one teaspoonful of Marmite went straight into his mouth. His cheeky look soon disappeared, his mouth dropped open and his eyes bulged as he ran outside to spit it out. "I'm going to die" he wailed, as he rolled up into a ball on the ground. We all thought it was hilarious, and offered him no sympathy at all.

After we had been at the Monastery for about 3 weeks, the boys asked us if we would like to go and see two horses kept about 300 metres from us. I couldn't believe it, I had not seen or heard any horses. We all set off down a track and came to an old barn; the owner was not around. "Never mind," said one of the boys, "I know a way in."

Feeling like children scrumping apples, we followed the boys around the back of the barn. "In here," they beckoned. We all scrambled through a broken window, into a very dark underground room, There, chained to the wall, were two Lusitano stallions. Apart from the little bit of light through the window, they were in complete darkness, they looked reasonably well fed, but there was no life in their eyes. I approached one, a white stallion, he was very nervous; he edged away from me as far as he could, but eventually allowed me to touch him. He was a beauty, and as I stroked his face, I looked into his eyes, and had a strong feeling that our paths would cross again.

We had been with the horses for quite a while when we heard a big sliding metal door being opened, which was the proper entry/exit point. We made a quick exit back the way we had come, and on the way back up the track, we bumped into the owner. He looked disapprovingly at the boys, but introduced himself to us, in English; of course he knew who we were, everyone in the area seemed to have heard of us!

CHAPTER 4

PIRI PIRI CHICKEN

Next morning we drove into Arganil for the weekly market day, where you can buy just about anything. There was a once a week bus service which ran up into the mountains, and for the people who live up in the little mountain villages, it was a lifeline. They came down into town in their best clothes, to gossip and sell any excess food. I'm sure in the olden days this would have included the odd goat or pig, but these days it's mainly vegetables. I remember buying fresh eggs and goat's cheeses from a sweet smiley little old lady. When I returned some years later, I asked her where her eggs and cheeses were. She told me EEC rules banned her from selling them. Then, lifting up a cotton cover from the basket on her lap, and with a beautiful twinkling smile, she asked what I would like? Inside the basket, were eggs and the little goat's cheeses I loved so much!

The barbecued piri piri chicken lunch at the market was the best I had ever tasted, everyone sat outside at long tables made from wooden planks that bent in the middle at the slightest pressure, the worn very old plastic stools wobbled on the dirt floor, but the atmosphere made up for the discomfort! The tarpaulin covered stall was a family affair, with the grandmother coating the chickens with a home made sauce as they spat and crackled on the barbecue. Wafts of smoke drifted over the hungry diners; she would never tell the recipe for her sauce; but it certainly included chillies! Steve had tried to worm it out of her, she gave him a small water bottle full of her concoction to take home but she would not tell her secrets.

Her son, the waiter, was a rotund, red-faced happy chap, with a joke and a smile for everyone. Other family members peeled potatoes (no frozen chips here) and prepared salad. During the school holidays the younger members of the family also helped, serving drinks. The skinny street dogs looked forward to market day too, gorging themselves on all the bones and leftovers.

We noticed smaller barbecues, literally two bricks with a rack across them, at ground level. We couldn't work out what they were for, until an old man bent down and lit one, then, taking out a few sardines from his bag, he cooked them himself above the fire. It seems it's perfectly legitimate to buy fresh fish from the market stalls, and cook it yourself if you don't fancy chicken! The wine flowed freely at 40 cents a litre and people swapped lively stories and gossiped in the smokey air.

Coming from England in November, with its storms and rain, we couldn't believe the wonderful warm weather. We went walking most days, exploring different tracks. We often followed the sound of water, and had found some lovely streams running through fields and woods. Craig and his new friend Jorge would jump in and swim in the freezing mountain water.

One day we heard a shout from Craig, "Look at this tree full of apples Dad." Steve went to investigate. He picked one, and noticed that the skin was leathery. Jorge took the fruit from Steve and smashed it on a rock, it split open and there on the ground was a walnut in its shell. Jorge broke the shell in his teeth and ate the nut. He grimaced and spat it out. "It's not ripe yet," said Steve, "It's all rubbery," the tree was obviously wild, so we picked a bagful to take home, "We'll keep them until Christmas" I said.

On the way home, we got lost and found ourselves walking up a very overgrown valley. We knew we were going in the wrong direction, but we could see what looked like a building ahead and were intrigued. We walked on and found overgrown vegetable patches, and other derelict buildings, only one of the buildings still had a roof, but the windows and doors had long since gone. It looked as if it was once a thriving village, but was now totally abandoned. I wondered where all the inhabitants had gone...and why. Jorge just shrugged when I asked him if he knew where all the inhabitants had gone, I would have to ask the older boys if they had an answer.

During our first few weeks at the college, we got on well with the little shepherd; our mutual love of animals seemed to transcend the language barrier. As time went on however it dawned on him that our horses were eating his flock's precious grass. He started to complain that the milk yield had dropped, and of our horses frightening his sheep, then one day Toby our dog, had a scuffle with his dog, which was a huge Serra da Estrela mountain dog. The little shepherd was furious, insisting that we keep Toby chained up.

Hilario called a meeting and explained to us that the main aim of the college was teaching young, would be farmers, how to look after land and animals to make a profit. It specialized in sheep farming; the riding school was secondary. As soon as the stables were finished, the horses would be expected to live inside, giving the field back to the shepherd. We told him we would think about it, but I already knew my answer.

We were still looking at properties, but had found nothing suitable, and although my command of the language was improving, it was still minimal. How could I teach Portuguese people to ride, when I could hardly speak the language? The sand arena where I would be expected to give riding lessons, was being built, but it was very small, I tried to imagine my horses trudging round and round this fenced arena in the hot summer sun. I didn't think they would be too keen! And as for having no freedom, having to spend 24 hours a day in a stable, never feeling the sun on their backs or rolling in mud, never tasting fresh spring grass, I couldn't do that to them, they loved their freedom, it would be like condemning them to life imprisonment. Poor Toby was also miserable, sulking on the end of his chain, his head between his paws; he looked up at us without even a thump of his tail.

Miguel came to visit us a few days later saying. "I have good news and bad news. First the bad news." We didn't know what to expect; everyone dreads bad news, but as he started talking, I felt a great weight being lifted from me. The decision was being made for us. Someone else had applied for the job of running the riding school, and reluctantly the college had decided to give him the job. It was the man with the two incarcerated horses down the track. We didn't argue, we already felt that this was the wrong place for us.

"What's the good news?" I asked, hardly able to contain my relief. "An acquaintance of mine" Miguel began, "is a council member for the town of Góis, about 15 kilometers away. I have been talking with him about you; he has some land available, and is keen to meet you. I'm having lunch with him today, so why don't you come along?"

"Yes Miguel, we have been to Góis, don't you remember, we stayed at the campsite when we were here in May," I reminded him.

"Oh yes, of course," he recalled. "Well, you can visit Roger and Peggy afterwards if you want to," he suggested.

"Yes, it would be lovely to see them, how was their first summer running the campsite"?

"Oh yes, they did really well," Miguel threw over his shoulder as he jumped into his car. He drove at his normal breakneck speed along a winding mountain road, we found it hard to keep up in our old Cavalier. As we rounded one bend we came face to face with a heavily loaded wood truck, forcing Steve to swerve to the outside edge of the road to avoid it. Luckily he kept his eyes fixed on the road but I couldn't help noticing the huge drop off with no barriers that could have been our fate. I'm sure that if I climbed down the escarpment I would find a graveyard of old battered cars; better not to know!

Finally we descended into a valley; late flowering heather blushed the mountains in the hazy winter sunshine, everywhere was so beautiful. We passed a large flat field of about 10 acres; "Wow look at that field, look at all that grass." I sighed.

We arrived in town and Miguel led us into what looked like a hole in the wall, like a cave, dark and gloomy, I could see that there were a few old men perched on stools with a bottle of wine on the bar, and one old man refilling his glass, noticed us coming in. His face lit up into a smile, "Miguel, como está?" (How are you?) There was much hand shaking and backslapping between all the men, "Quer vinho?" (You want wine?) "Sim, se faz favor," (yes please,) we all answered. The bartender brought more glasses and the old man poured us all a glass of wine from his bottle. While Miguel was talking with the man, whom he introduced as his great uncle, our interest had been piqued by some large round cheeses in one corner. The bartender asked if we would like to try a piece. We were both lovers of cheese, and were soon conversing with him on the qualities of each one. Some of them were from his herd of goats, very matured and quite expensive; we decided to treat ourselves to a small piece from three different ones.

Delicious smells were coming from the next room; through the door, I could see a huge pan simmering away, and another with trout simmering in what smelt like vinegar. The cook, noticing me, beckoned me in; I asked what was in the pan "Feijoada," came the reply; it looked like a bean soup with rice and pork. I noticed some strange looking cuts of meat floating about, and he laughed at the distasteful look on my face as it dawned on me why he was holding onto his ear and pointing to his feet! It smelt delicious, but I couldn't, I just couldn't.

A tall younger man, smartly dressed in a suit, entered the bar, Miguel introduced us to Roberto, and together we walked through to the dining area, which was better lit, but very small, just one large table and two smaller ones. Steve and I both decided to order the trout, which was so tasty that we asked the cook for the recipe to try at home.

Roberto was a charming man, who spoke good English. He liked the idea of having a riding school in his town, but the council had no funds to help us. We were again unsure about having a riding school, but, as with many other things in life, we realized that we might have to compromise. At least this would be our school, run on our terms.

After lunch, he took us to see the land; Quinta da Ribeira had been a cow farm many years ago. It was the ten acres that I had seen from the car. It was nice flat land, but no fencing that I could see, or electricity or water. Roberto promised that he would arrange for the water supply to be reconnected, and he left us there to explore. From the road, the land had looked lovely, but now standing there, we could see that the long grass hid the fact that it had been roughly ploughed, then left to nature. Brambles reigned, their thorns digging into us from every direction as we fought our way through. Finally we came out on the other side of the property, and found a little brick built house, right on the main road. There were steps leading from the little house, down to the fields. The roof of the house was sagging a bit but there was a large barn next to it that was in quite good condition. Next to the house was a concrete parking area, which extended out over the land below, supported by concrete pillars. Immediately we saw the potential for three stables underneath.

Suddenly an old woman appeared with a key in her hand. She gestured with her hands, that we could come and look inside. The door opened on to a room full of seed potatoes that were covered in a poisonous dust to deter rats. It smelt awful! A mixture of old rotten potatoes, chemicals and mouldy wood! We thanked her and quickly retreated into the fresh air. The room we had just entered was on road level; we suspected that there was another floor underneath, cut out of the rock.

We walked down the flight of stone steps, and, hidden by a 10-foot wall of brambles, we could just make out a door. This project was going to be a big challenge, but we decided there and then to have a go.

A couple of days later, we went to see Roberto at his offices, to talk more, but he was not available; we talked with his assistant in Portuguese. We *thought* he said we could have a contract for 5 or 10 years, we *thought* he said we could gut the house, and make a cozy cottage for ourselves; he seemed to smile and agree with everything we said! We made out a plan of what we intended to do; build a sand school, fence some land for grazing, build 3 stables under the forecourt, and if possible, do up the house. He said, he would show it at the next meeting of the council, and let us know. He was happy for us to start fencing straight away.

We left the meeting that day feeling daunted by the work, but happy. Steve remembered seeing a wood yard in Arganil, we needed a big pile of posts for fencing, so the next day we paid a visit. The owner of the wood yard was a gregarious man with a big smile and a belly to match. His jowly face sported the most lustrous black moustache I had seen in a long time! He shook our hands vigorously, and introduced himself as Eduardo. The workforce was mainly women who were chipping the bark from newly cut pine trees. Their hands and clothing were black from the resin, it looked like a horrible job; but they were chatting and laughing as they toiled. An old transistor radio was blaring out over the whine of the machines that were milling the wood. Steve told Eduardo he needed about 200 posts; Eduardo threw his hands in the air; "No problem he said, "I will bring them tomorrow." Next we visited a hardware shop and bought wire, nails, two enxadas, and a foice roçadeira. An enxada is an essential tool; everybody has one. It is like a hoe but has a straight edge for digging the rocky soil. The Portuguese seem to be able to use this one tool for just about everything. A foice roçadeira is a vicious looking hook on the end of a four-foot handle, used for slashing at brambles and saplings. I was to become very familiar with the foice roçadeira over the next few weeks!

Sure enough Eduardo arrived next morning, he had driven the 15 kilometres of narrow windy mountain roads, on his tractor with a trailer full of wooden posts. He helped us unload: "Anything else you need-just call me" he shouted as he set off on a 15k trip back home.

We decided to fence in two acres of the best land, which was at the back of the house. Steve set about digging 80 post holes, (luckily he had brought his post hole shovel with him from England) each about 75cm deep, whilst Craig and I declared war on the brambles. We soon had the frontage at the lower level cleared, and we found two more rooms. They had once housed goats and other livestock; the old bedding was still down on the floor. Rats, mice, and the biggest spiders I have ever seen, were now the only inhabitants!

There were about 30 olive trees on the land. After each olive harvest, the trees are heavily pruned. The branches had been left lying where they had fallen, and over the years had accumulated. They posed a danger in a field where horses were to graze, so we had to clear them. What with all these branches and bundle upon bundle of bramble cuttings, we kept a bonfire going for two weeks! The remaining 8 acres looked much more formidable, parts of it looked as if it was used as a dumping ground. We would just concentrate on the two acres behind the house for the moment.

We worked until dark every day before making the half hour drive up winding mountain roads, back to the caravan, to feed the horses and ourselves. Steve's hands were blistered from digging holes and humping heavy 4"x4" wooden posts. Craig and I had torn, weeping fingers from fighting the battle of the brambles. Toby, who had been coming with us every day, had made the most of his freedom, snuffling through the long grass looking for mice, or rabbits. His poor nose was so sore it bled, but still he carried on snuffling, earning himself the nickname of 'The Snufflehound'. Things were taking shape, the fences were built, the lower rooms of the house, which we planned to use as stables, to start with, were cleaned out. We started to plan our second move.

The horses were reluctant to go back into their horsebox prison, I can't say I blamed them, and anyway we thought it would be fun to ride them the 15 kilometers to their new home. The day before we planned to leave, Guv lost a shoe. Now we would have to delay the move and find a farrier. We were in town that afternoon when we bumped into Miguel. We had been trying to make our own way a bit, and not rely on him for everything; he was always so busy. I just mentioned in conversation that Guv had lost a shoe. "Well, what a coincidence," he said, "only half an hour ago I saw a man riding a horse through the town, I stopped him to have a chat, and mentioned you two and your horses. I jotted down his number somewhere, yes, here it is, give him a ring, he speaks English."

Steve phoned him from a café. Albino did know of a farrier; he would call round the next day and take us to his house. He arrived in a 4-wheel drive jeep. After introductions, we all piled in and set off along dirt tracks, heading up into the mountains. The day was clear and sunny, the main track that we were traveling along was criss-crossed with smaller tracks. As we went higher, the trees were less dense, giving way to the most breathtaking views of mist shrouded mountains. We could just make out the slopes of the Serra de Estrela which at 2000 metres is the highest mountain range in Portugal.

Albino stopped the jeep, and we all got out. We had our maps with us; Albino pointed out where we were, and the names of the villages below us. We were at about 900 meters; the air was so fresh and clean. Birds of prey were circling above us, the long winter grass swaying slightly in the gentle breeze, the sweet smell of late flowering heather hanging heavily in the air. "This would be a lovely place to come on horseback," I enthused, "We could all ride up here together one day," said Albino, "I'd like to try your thoroughbred!"

"That would be great, I'd love it." I said enthusiastically. "That village down there is where we are heading," he said, getting back into the jeep. We all followed, and set off down the steep stony track.

We drove up the cobbled street of a very old village. Some of the houses were abandoned, no more than ruins, all of them looked very rustic, chickens were running in the road, and skinny dogs sniffed nervously at our heels; the houses were all made of slate and mud, with wooden shutters. Albino rapped on an open door, and called out "Antonio, Antonio." A small (I was beginning to realize that these mountain folk are all small!) squat man of about 60 years, appeared from the dark smokey room. Surely this can't be the farrier, I thought, but as we were ushered into the room, it was immediately obvious that he was. Every corner of the room was piled high with metal shoes, but what struck me was that all the shoes were small.

Albino chatted to the little guy, explaining our problem then turned to us to translate. "He has only ever shod donkeys and cows, but as long as your horse is well behaved, he is willing to give it a try."

"What about your horses?" I asked feeling slightly alarmed, "who shoes them?"

"I have only had my horses for a month, and so far they haven't needed to be re-shod, I will be interested to see what sort of a job he does," he said, totally oblivious to my rising panic. Guv was to be the guinea pig.

Antonio was giving a very quick wash to a grimy little glass, before filling it to the brim from a dusty old barrel and handing it to Steve. Not being much of a drinker especially during the day, he tried to refuse, but realizing that it was the old boy's home made wine, and not wanting to offend him; he took a swig. I could tell from Steve's expression, and bulged out cheeks, that his taste buds did not appreciate the assault! As soon as the glass was empty, Antonio took it from him and eagerly went to refill it. "Nao, nao, faz favor, chega" (No, no - please, it's enough) Steve pleaded.

Next the refilled glass was handed to Albino; he was obviously a bit more wily. After the smallest sip, he assured Antonio that it was one of the best wines he had ever tasted, but he was the driver and had to keep a clear head. Antonio took the glass from Albino, and emptied it straight down his throat, saying, "If one dies, we all die!" Was he referring to the wine I wondered? I was glad that as a female, I was not required to go through this ritual.

Antonio did not have a shoe anywhere near the size for Guv, so we decided that if we all spread out across the horse's field, and systematically searched, we should find the lost shoe. He brought all his tools; I was amazed to see that he had the same nails, special ones from Sweden that my farrier used in England.

Eventually we found the shoe, and led Guv onto a flat piece of ground. Now he was confronted by this huge horse, I could see poor Antonio was quavering in his boots, but Guv was a very kind gentle horse, and soon the shoe was securely back on his hoof. In England the work would have cost me at least £10, the old man didn't want to charge us, maybe he was hoping for more work in the future. When we insisted on paying him something for his trouble, he asked for the equivalent of 40 pence. We gave him about £5; he was happy and so were we.

Albino ran Antonio back home, and I wondered if he would escape a drinking session as easily this time. Although he did a good job of putting on one shoe, Antonio was puffing and sweating, I couldn't imagine him coping with 3 horses, that's eleven more hooves!

CHAPTER 5

NEW YEAR'S EVE PARTY

Early next morning, we saddled up the horses, and set off to ride to their new home. We guessed it would take us about 3 hours riding, plus an hour for a couple of stops. We were in no hurry - we had all day. Steve had studied our newly acquired military maps, and found a route that kept us on tracks for nearly the whole way. We packed our saddle bags with food and drink for a picnic, mainly for Craig's sake, he was only 9 years old, and not used to riding for so long.

On route, I began to see the opportunities for riding holidays. The rugged, diverse beauty of the mountains would surely appeal to horse lovers back home, some of whom only had contact with horses once a week for lessons at a riding school. Riding outside of an arena is so different, I really felt at one with Roxy, he was enjoying himself too; how wonderful it would be to earn a living, doing what I enjoyed most!

We rode through a lovely village called Celavisa; Most of the houses had balconies adorned with a dazzling array of colour. Geraniums, and other English summer blooms were still flowering, clumps of arum lilies were growing along the riverbank some already in flower. The enticing aroma of sardines being cooked on an outdoor grill drifted towards us. Goats bleated and dogs barked, chickens scattered as the hooves of the horses clattered down the cobbled street. People came out of their homes to see the commotion; most had never seen a horse up close, everyone was so enthusiastic and curious, we were offered wine, water for our horses, even biscuits! Roxy caught the smell of the sweet biscuits, and stopping in his tracks, he reached out his long neck looking for a tit-bit from the woman holding the packet. She was petrified and dropping the packet, she ran back to the safety of her house! A brave little girl picked up the packet, and shared them out between the three horses; people were stroking them, and asking so many questions. Where were we going? What did they eat? But we didn't want to stop too long; we still had a way to go.

When we finally arrived at Quinta da Ribeira, our new home, the old woman (with the key) was storing her potatoes into sacks. She stopped and gave us a toothless smile, and turned back to her task; each time she tossed a potato into the sack, a cloud of dust from the rat poison, rose up into the air, and I was horrified to see her hands were covered in it. I tried to draw her attention to the fact, but she gave a dismissive wave of her hand, "Nao faz mal," she said in her guttural mountain dialect, which directly translates as; doesn't make bad, but it means; "It doesn't matter."

We took off the saddles and bridles, and led the horses down to their new field; it looked very posh with the new wooden fencing. We had been advised to use old engine oil, as a cheap alternative to wood preserver. The local garage had given us a huge tub of it, and I had painted all the wood to protect it from the dreaded wood beetle, and also supposedly to keep moisture out. The dirty black oil darkened the new pine, but the overall effect was very nice. The horses were not concerned with the colour of the fencing, they were very appreciative of the new field, but it was the grass they were more interested in! After a luxurious roll to rid themselves of the feeling of having us on their backs for so long, down went their heads to graze.

The old lady lifted the last sack of potatoes into her squeaky rusty old wheelbarrow, and handed us the key, before trundling off down the road. We now had to get ourselves back to the Monastery to pick up all our vehicles. A large truck was approaching; Steve stepped out and put up his thumb. Hitch hiking was very common here, children often hitched to and from school. The bus service was almost non-existent, so you either hitched or walked! The driver stopped. "Arganil faz favor," shouted Steve. "Sim," he replied nodding his head with a smile; we all jumped up into the cab, he even drove three kilometres out of his way to drop us at the door of the Monastery.

We said our goodbyes to everyone, we had become quite friendly with some of the staff, even the little shepherd seemed sad to see us leaving. He gave me a present of some wild mushrooms he had picked that morning. The three boys promised to keep in touch. "It will be dull here without you, and your horses," said Jorge sulking. "Come and visit us anytime," I said sadly, "We're not that far away." The journey back was uneventful. We drove all the vehicles down into the field we were to share with the horses, unhitched the caravans, and then parked the truck and car up on the forecourt. One animal who was very happy to leave the college was Toby. No more chains, he had complete freedom now, he could snuffle until his nose could stand it no more!

Roxy also liked having us living in his field, he soon formed a habit of waking us up in the morning by pushing himself against the caravan, making it move a bit. "Come on wake up," he was saying! The windows were hinged at the top, opening outwards, he would wait for me to open my window in the morning, and by contorting his head and neck sideways, he could reach into the caravan and eat toast from my plate! During the daytime, when the door was open, he would poke his head in, to see what we were doing. Luckily the door was too narrow for his shoulders to fit; otherwise I'm sure he would have come right inside.

We had none of our former luxuries now, like toilet and shower facilities, or electricity. Steve dug a deep hole in the ground, and we erected our little toilet tent over it for privacy. He had roughed it a few times before, but for Craig and I, this was a first. He disregarded our moans, saying it was much better for the environment, and for your thigh muscles!

Christmas was approaching, Paul and Mella, my older children, were flying out to be with us. I could not wait to see the look on Mella's face, when I showed her the bathroom. Being a teenager, she was fond of preening herself for hours, what would she and Paul think? We had bought a large gas lamp, which lit the caravan sufficiently, and put up a little Christmas tree, but it looked a bit drab without any lights. Craig decorated it with tinsel and glass baubles, and laid presents out beneath it. We were all excited about seeing Paul and Mella, although we had only left England two months before; it seemed like a lifetime, so much had happened. We were a close family, and had not been parted for so long before.

I watched the strangers' faces filing into the arrivals hall, eager to recognize their loved ones. Then we spotted our own, Paul first, with his 6ft frame and long curly hair, how could we miss him. Mella was beside him, anxiously searching for our faces in the crowd. There were hugs and kisses all round, with lots of chatter and excitement, as we made our way home.

I was a little worried that they would be shocked by our standard of living, but I need not have worried, they fell in love with the place at first sight. They thought the toilet was hilarious and fought over who would try it first. We had a lovely family Christmas, the last all together for a long time. They brought parcels from all the family in England, my brother even thought to send some Christmas crackers!

Christmas day was typical for December; cold and frosty mornings with gloriously warm afternoons, plummeting to freezing nights. This warm sunny Christmas afternoon, we decided to go and explore the mountains. We drove the car to the lower reaches, and then walked. We came upon a lovely little village called Pena, tucked away in the shadows of a huge craggy mountain. There was a small river running alongside, boulders had rolled down the mountain in the past and lodged themselves into the river, making large stepping-stones.

We all had wellies on, so decided to follow the river a little way. Paul and Craig went on ahead. They called themselves the 'Great explorers',and re-named themselves Plophead the Navigator and Indiana Windhead! They crossed the river, it was quite dangerous, some of the boulders were huge and very slippery. On the other side, they found some abandoned houses and an old water mill. They were beckoning us to follow them, but I was a bit dubious, the water looked icy cold. Steve went first, precariously tackling the rocks. I followed behind, and Mella brought up the rear. Toby made it all look so easy, jumping athletically from rock to rock. Some boulders were covered in black ice, where the sun had not reached. Mella found this out for herself. She slipped and fell, just holding on with her fingertips, there was another rock just three inches from her feet, we urged her to let herself drop the three inches, but she would not loosen her grip, she just clung there begging for help.

I was nearest to her, so I retraced my steps to help her. I slipped on the very same rock, and fell into the freezing water. Luckily it was not too deep, but it came over the top of my boots, I was soaked! Mella in a fit of laughter released her grip of the rock and landed safely on the rock below. Everyone had a good laugh at my expense, but I insisted we go home; I was frozen.

Back at the caravan, I boiled some water, and soaked my feet. Oh what bliss! It was only then that I saw the funny side of it.

One morning we went to visit Roger and Peggy at the campsite. They had already been here for nine months, and were settling down to the slow easy way of the Portuguese. They were enjoying their new life, and gave us advice on many things, but best of all, they asked us if we would like to use of their showers. We all accepted gratefully and the indulgence of a weekly hot shower was wonderful. The rest of the week it was a choice of a bowl of hot water, or, Paul and Craig the 'great explorers' had found a lovely little stream on the edge of our land. It was about knee deep, but very cold. Sometimes on a warm afternoon, they would take a dip, but it was not until the end of March that I slowly, and painfully ventured in with my bar of soap!

A couple of days after Christmas, we heard a motorbike approaching; I looked out of the caravan to see a man lifting his helmet off his head. "Hi, are you English?" he said, in English! He came as quite a shock; it hadn't occurred to us that other English people would be living here. "I noticed your English plated vehicles. And thought I would come and say hello," he said cheerfully. "Come in," I said, happy to be able to speak my own language. "Have a drink." We sat chatting for a while and it turned out that he had a holiday home about 10 miles away, he invited us to a New Year's Eve party that was being held near to him and gave us directions. Next day whilst shopping, we met another English couple, who only lived 10 minutes from us; obviously we were not as clever as we thought and we were not the only foreigners to have found this beautiful area! Sam and Jacky were going to the party too, so we arranged to go with them.

The party was held in a huge rambling old house, with cellars below, and surrounded by a beautiful old wooden veranda. The courtyard had been covered in tarpaulins, because it was raining. A naked guy sporting only horns on his head and a goat's skull for a codpiece met us at the door...Quite a culture shock! A reggae band was playing on the veranda, people were dancing in the courtyard, nearly everyone was in fancy dress, I felt dowdy in my raincoat. There were jugglers, fire-eaters, people twirling fluorescent ribbons, it was a really eclectic mix of nations from all over the world.

We learned that this venue was the 'in' place to be on New Year's Eve and people travelled from all over Europe to this beautiful old farm in the middle of the Portuguese countryside to party the night away and welcome in the New Year.

Two sisters and their families owned the farm. One of the sisters called Dennie had two sons of Craig's age. She invited Craig to go into the house, and play Lego with her boys, we tried to encourage him, but he was too shy, he wouldn't go.

We were all having a really good time, dancing and meeting new people, when one of the tarpaulins collapsed under the weight of the heavy rain. Poor Craig took an unexpected cold shower! He was right underneath it. Dennie almost immediately appeared with a towel, dry clothes and a blanket to wrap him in. A firework display had been organized, but it fizzled in the rain, so after wishing Happy New Year to numerous new friends, we all left the party which looked set to go on all night.

I was disappointed that Craig had been too shy to make new friends, but he would have another chance I was sure. Three days later the dreaded day loomed. School. He had picked up some basic language, but nothing could have prepared him for his first day at school. Before the Christmas holidays, we had visited the school with Craig. One teacher spoke a little English, so it was decided that he should go into her class. She had never taught a foreigner before and was apprehensive herself. Craig had seemed quite cool about starting, but looking back now, I think he just shut it from his mind.

When he was finally faced with leaving home, he burst into tears, and sobbed, desperately clinging to me and begging me not to send him. It was terrible, my stomach was churning, I had a huge lump in my throat, I was crying with him, but he had to go. Steve, seeing my state decided to take him alone. He was still pleading not to go, as Steve led him to the car. When they had gone, I burst into floods of tears. What had we done? How could we do it to him? We should never have come here; it was all a mistake.

Steve returned upset, he said Craig could not stop himself from crying in front of his teacher and the children. He was not a little boy of five just starting school, he was a big boy of nine, crying in front of a class of foreigners. Steve said the teacher had been wonderful, taking him into her arms and hugging him, all the children surrounded him wanting to be his friend.

I could not be placated, and wandered around all day in a dream, thinking of him facing the most difficult day of his young life. I waited for his return with a heavy heart, thinking we would have to go through this again tomorrow.

Steve went to collect him at the end of the day, and they both came back smiling. Would you believe, he had enjoyed it. He said it was OK; he had made friends, and didn't mind going again tomorrow. We had all overcome our first big obstacle. From that day on, Craig loved his school, and within a year, he was speaking the language fluently. We were also now having Portuguese lessons with a lovely girl who was training to be a language teacher. At last we were beginning to make progress!

CHAPTER 6

PAUL'S PADDOCK

January 1995...Just before Mella was due to return to England, we decided to have a family day out riding. We had bought Craig a mountain bike for Christmas, so he and Steve went on bikes, Paul rode Guv, Mella rode Smartie, and I rode Roxy. Toby trotted along beside us; sometimes zigzagging off into the woods, on the trail of a rabbit, which he never managed to catch! We had planned a route of about 8 kilometres in a direction that we had not explored before.

After about 3k, we came upon a house; it was just off the country lane that we were riding along, standing all by itself surrounded by forest. "Oh look," Steve exclaimed, "What a beautiful house. If I could choose a place to live, this would be it." It certainly was lovely, built of river boulders, it looked very old, but the roof looked in good condition and the land around the house had been strimmed. Someone obviously lived there. Suddenly Mella said, "I can hear water, yes, look, I can see it sparkling through the trees." Sure enough, there was a large river flowing only 50 metres away. I could not see any electricity posts or wires, or phones lines; whoever lived there led a very simple existence; but what a spectacular setting.

We all enjoyed our last ride together, and the next day we set off to take Mella to the airport. I was going to miss her a lot, but she would be back for the whole of the summer. She was just starting college in London and was moving into a flat with a friend. She was apprehensive about us being so far away, and so was I, but we would write every week and if she had a problem she could phone Peggy the Belgian lady at the campsite and she would get a message to us.

Paul, was to stay on until June; he had a summer job lined up in Brighton as a beach lifeguard, a job that suited him down to the ground. He was a real Bay Watch type character, (and why not at 21 years old) Paul was always testing his strength, lifting heavy objects, he was proud of his physique. A British friend called Geoff who we had met at the New Year's Eve party, was building a house nearby, he offered Paul some labouring work. Geoff nicknamed him 'Iron Man'! Paul had only ever worked out in gyms, he had never done a proper day's labouring in his life. After a few day's work, he started to complain about aching muscles, bad back, blistered feet, etc. etc. Our friend on paying him for his work, made us all laugh, he re-named him 'Plasticine Man'. The name has stuck to this day.

Paul, having an outgoing personality, needed the company of other young people. He started cycling into Góis, to have a beer in the evenings. Before long, he had a group of Portuguese friends, and was learning the language really fast. Blonde hair and blue eyes are uncommon here; he was very popular with the girls! Some of Paul's new friends worked in the forests, felling eucalyptus trees. He needed money, and arranged to work with them. Just after 6 am, one freezing morning, he walked the 2 miles to the point where he would be picked up, we didn't see him again until he staggered in exhausted at 9pm; and went straight to bed. Next morning I tentatively asked him how his day had been. "Never again, never again," he repeated.

He told me while rubbing his blistered hands that the group of five workers were picked up at 7am, and driven to a forest, where the boss dropped them all off and went away. Paul worked hard all day with just an axe, his job was to chop off the smaller branches of the trees that were being felled. He found it hard to keep up with the Portuguese workers who did this sort of work everyday, it was relentless but his pride kept him going. The boss finally returned at 6.00pm. It was already dark, and they were all cold and hungry, yet even on the drive home, the boss stopped at a bar to make a phone call, then stopped at a friend's house for 20 minutes, leaving them sitting in the truck outside. The other lads accepted it as normal; they said they were just pleased to have some work. When the boss paid Paul the equivalent of about £10 for his efforts, he said he felt like throwing it at him, but he refrained.... £10 could buy a lot of beer! "Never mind." I said, making him a cup of tea. "We have a job for you now."

Roxy was beginning to get on our nerves, he was always craning his head into the caravan to see what we were doing, at first it was funny, but now it was raining, and the field around the caravan had turned to mud, because the horses, mainly Roxy, were always standing there looking for tit bits.

We had erected an awning, to store the bikes, vegetables, dog food etc. in a dry place. One day whilst we were out, Roxy had ripped open the canvas door, and come inside the awning, eaten all of the carrots, apples, cabbage, and anything else edible, leaving only the garlic and onions untouched. Once inside, and stomach full, he tried to turn around to get out. He must have got stuck and panicked, because he managed to bend all the poles and almost knock down the whole awning, trampling on sacks of dog food, old saucepans, and other knick-knacks, in a demolition derby of destruction!

We decided that a second paddock with a separate gate would give us more privacy. It would also give the grass in the first paddock time to recover, and hopefully help dry up the mud. The second paddock would be Paul's job. He set to work digging holes for the posts, it was hard going because the ground was often frosted up in the mornings, but to his credit, he persevered, and 'Paul's paddock' began to take shape.

Steve was building a sand school, and he needed someone with a tractor to come and plough up a square of land. One of the locals had offered to do it, so one afternoon, Steve and Paul set off for his house to arrange it. Now visiting a Portuguese person's house is very dangerous, but my two men were innocents in those days. The locals love to play the game 'let's get the estrangeiro (foreigner) drunk!' A group of locals had gathered for the event, and Steve and Paul were like lambs to the slaughter; they had no chance! They staggered home hours later, giggling and slurring their words. Paul had a bottle clasped tightly in his hand. "Try some of this," he giggled, "it will blow your head off."

"That stuff could launch a rocket," slurred Steve, his knees buckling as he collapsed onto the sofa. I put the coffee pot on.

"It wasn't just us that got caught," said Steve sobering slightly, "Sam was there as well, he invited us to a barbecue at his place tomorrow."

"What about the tractor man?" I asked, thinking the whole thing was very funny; I had never seen Steve drunk before. "Oh yes, he's coming tomorrow morning," he slurred.

Another thing that we had to learn was the word amanhã. In the dictionary it is stated as meaning tomorrow, but in real life it is totally open ended. It can mean next week, next month, next year, but very rarely tomorrow.

Sure enough tomorrow dawned without any sign of the tractor man. On our way up to Sam and Jacky's house, we stopped to ask him why he hadn't come. His list of excuses were endless, his wife was ill, he had to look after the children, his tractor wouldn't start, he would have to fix it. Anything but admit he probably had a stonking hangover!

Sam and Jacky lived in a pretty little cottage, half way up the mountain. There were three or four other houses nearby, but it was quite remote and very beautiful. We had a few good barbecues up there during January when the sun shone. We felt smug as we thought of folks back home, huddled around their central heating. Sitting outside eating good food, drinking wine, and watching the sun set over the mountains was quite magical.

Sam asked us if we would be prepared to move into their cottage for a month, to look after their cats while they went back to England to do some visiting. We jumped at the chance; they had a bathroom, plumbed in water, electricity, and to Craig's delight, a TV – what luxury! Paul, who had made our little caravan his own, was also drawn by the TV. He joined us in the cottage, watching films all night, and then refusing to get up to work next morning. Who would have thought that only 3 months before, we had taken all these things for granted – never again. The first thing I did was to soak in a hot bath scented with essential oils. Steve soon returned to his old habit of sitting on the toilet reading a magazine, something you cannot comfortably do whilst squatting over a hole in the ground! We took Craig down the mountain to school each day, it was about 3 kilometres of steep downhill. Of course this meant that at the end of the day, the children who lived in the mountain villages around Sam and Jacky's cottage, had to walk 3kilometres up a very steep hill, to get home. We passed a group of about six children with rucksacks full of books, just starting the ascent. We screeched to a halt and offered some of them a lift. They all clambered in! How could we leave some behind? it would have been cruel. Craig jumped into the front on my lap, and all six children squashed onto the back seat, throwing their rucksacks in the boot, which we only just managed to force shut. This quickly became the norm ... our poor old car would struggle back up the hills each evening, crammed with excitable children. The month passed too quickly, and we were soon back in the caravan.

Jacky introduced me to a friend of hers who wanted to do some riding. Sarah was an excellent rider who instantly formed a good relationship with Smartie, who was a sensitive little Arab, and a real joy to ride; she started coming every Sunday morning. We went out together into the mountains, neither of us had any sense of direction; we were always getting lost!

One frosty Sunday morning, we set off to ride to the top of our closest mountain called Serra do Rabadão. After a few wrong turns and dead end tracks, we reached the top. The horses were blowing hard after the climb, so we stopped at the top to give them a rest. The views were wonderful, stretching out into the clear sunny air, we were on a ridge track so had views in all directions. To the left, I could see Monte Alto where I had ridden with Carlos and Nuno in our first few weeks at Arganil. It was at least 12 kilometres away, yet it felt as though I could almost touch it. To the right I looked down on clusters of small villages; smoke rising from their chimneys. Ahead of me the mountains loomed into the distance; rather bleak except for their snow capped tops. We made a pact to return in the springtime when we thought this vast area would be abundant with wild flowers. The horses were very fresh, they soon got their breath back, and were fidgeting and tossing their heads. Roxy was just looking for trouble; swirling around, doing little half rears; trying to unseat me and loosen the reins so that he could gallop off. The track along the top was wide and because of recent rain, the sun softened frosty surface was good for a gallop. The horses were thinking the same thoughts. "Shall we have a gallop Sarah?" She didn't have time to answer; the horses were off! Oh, the exhilaration as we raced neck and neck across the top of the mountain ridge, which was about 800 metres above sea level. Tears streamed from my eyes, and my cheeks burnt from the cold air. I tried to drink in the views, but it was impossible at that speed and with Roxy's mane whipping my face.

After about half a mile, Roxy, with his heavier build, was blowing hard, but Smartie's Arab blood meant he could have kept on running. We pulled up for a breather and tried to get our bearings. We could see tiny villages far below us, the people going about their business looked like ants. We could have turned back, but I was not sure we would be able to find the small, heavily wooded track that we had come up by. We decided, or rather the horses decided we were going on. They were really excited now. Roxy was half rearing on the spot and his reins were slippery with sweat. "OK let's go!" The track switch-backed up and down a little, but the horses didn't seem to notice or slow their pace, we were all enjoying ourselves too much.

In general the tracks here are stony and hard, and although there are a few tracks suitable for cantering, this was our first gallop in Portugal. We must have covered at least 5 kilometres, sometimes walking to give the horses a breather, but mostly at gallop. It was wonderful, but we were becoming a bit apprehensive as to where we were going. Where would this track lead? It looked as if it went on for ever.

We needed to be heading downwards into the villages to return home. On rounding a bend, we found what we were looking for. Below us was a clearing, with tracks running off in all directions, and yes, one of them lead down. There was a water fountain at the clearing, what was that doing up here on the mountaintop? Later, I asked a Portuguese historian friend about the water fountain: "Oh yes," he replied, "you must have been on the pilgrim's trail, it goes all the way to Spain."

We rode down through a small village where people were working in the fields. We stopped and asked an old lady wearing a very wide brimmed straw hat for directions to Góis, which was the nearest town to us. She pointed reassuringly in the direction we were heading. Feeling happier now, we settled down for a long walk home. We were on a little tarmac road but not a single car passed us on the whole route. It wound down into a valley, then on through three or four delightful little villages. Church bells were ringing through the clear air, we could hear them all around us, some loud and close by and others from further away, all ringing out the hour at slightly different times and in slightly different tones, making it sound like a harmony.

Goats grazed on the hillside, their bells clinking around their necks. Chickens squawked at us in disgust and fluttered away. An old dog begrudgingly lifted himself from the warm tarmac to allow us to pass. A bubbling little stream followed us down from the mountain, and now ran through the middle of the villages in the valley. Each village had a little bridge to allow the inhabitants to cross from one side to the other. Waterfalls cascaded; their droplets sparkling in the low February sunshine. Everything around us was at peace with nature. We returned home very tired but inwardly refreshed.

A Portuguese friend of Paul's asked if he could accompany Sarah and I sometimes on our Sunday rides. Pedro had a great knowledge of the area, so he was very welcome. He had ridden as a teenager and competed in jumping competitions, but hadn't ridden for about 5 years. When I introduced him to Guv, he was really taken aback. "Wow! What a beautiful horse" he said; patting Guv's neck. "I have never ridden an English thoroughbred before, what a long neck he has compared to Portuguese Lusitano horses, I bet he has a great gallop!"

"Oh yes," I replied proudly. "He is actually Irish and raced in Ireland until he had an accident at the age of seven. But because he had such a wonderful temperament, the racing yard decided to give him a year off to recover. His racing name was 'KnowhatImean' but the stable girls who looked after him called him Guv, which relates to the Cockney saying 'Know what I mean Guv'. Once he recovered he was sold to an English jockey who raced Point-to-Point".

"What's Point-to-Point"? asked Pedro intrigued.

"It's amateur racing; usually over a course of about 3 miles and 18 brushwood fences. It always attracts a big crowd and is an exciting day out. People bet on which horse will win." I had to explain what a brushwood fence was because they don't have steeplechase racing here in Portugal. "Would you tell me Guv's story? I would love to hear it". We were waiting for Sarah to arrive so I was happy to recite his story.

"Okay" I began. "At that time I was very keen on Cross Country jumping, and had entered a competition riding my friend's horse Dandy. Also at the competition was a lady called Stephanie and her horse Guv. She told me that her husband rode Guv at Point-to-Point meetings but because he worked full time, it was her job to keep Guv fit during the week. Stephanie and her husband were trying for a baby and had been talking about selling Guv as she would not be able to ride him regularly once pregnant. Stephanie and Guv actually won the competition, but I didn't see her again until a few months later. She was pregnant and looking for a new home for Guv. I had been very taken by him and although we were making plans to move to Portugal, I arranged to go to her farm and try him out with the view to buy him." Pedro was keen to hear more.

"Go on" he coaxed.

"I arrived at her farm and had arranged for a local vet to come and examine Guv to make sure that he was fit and healthy. Stephanie explained to me that Guv had no shoes on, and had not been ridden in weeks so he was unfit. She said it would be unfair on him to expect too much from the vet's inspection and that she couldn't ride him as she was pregnant. I had seen him in action at the cross country show so I knew his capabilities.

"OK" I said,"I will be happy to just walk and trot him for the vet's inspection, and I will be happy to ride him." Just at that moment, the vet's four wheel drive came up the lane. A young good looking man came towards us with his hand outstretched.

"Hi, I'm David, this must be Guv." He checked Guv over from teeth to hooves. Then he watched him walk and trot with me leading him. So far-so-good; David seemed impressed. He asked to see him ridden so we tacked him up and I jumped on board. That was when the fun started!

"What happened" Pedro implored.

" Well" I chuckled. "After Stephanie had gone to great lengths to tell me that Guv had no shoes on so he was a bit footsore and also very unfit, David asked to see Guv ridden at a faster pace so that he could check his heart rate. I waited for her to explain to David that Guv was not fit enough to do the test, but she was nodding her head and agreeing with David that I should ride Guv faster at canter. She started chasing us around a very small arena brandishing a stick and shouting "Canter, Canter, Canter."

"Poor Guv" I explained to Pedro "had probably never been schooled; racehorses were very rarely schooled in those days, they only knew how to gallop in a straight line. He was a big horse and didn't really know how to cope with being chased around in a tiny arena so he did the only thing open to him...he bucked me off!"

Pedro thought it was hilarious, "What happened next" he wanted to know.

"Well as you can imagine, Stephanie was devastated; they both rushed over to see if I was okay. Luckily, I was fine. Of course, she thought she had lost her sale and said rather lamely that she had never known him to buck before; not expecting me to believe her. But I liked this horse and wanted to give him another chance. I asked her if she would agree to me taking Guv home with me on a month's loan, so that I could be sure the bucking was just a 'one off'. Stephanie jumped at the chance and so Guv came home with me and had never put a hoof wrong since. "In fact he's wonderful" I gushed, burying my face in his long black mane.

" I hope I haven't put you off of riding him?" I asked Pedro tentatively.

"Oh god no...not a bit" he laughed. "Shall I groom him and get his saddle on?"

"Yes sure, I can see Sarah just getting out of her car so I will start grooming Smartie for her" I said. We both greeted Sarah, and within 15 minutes we were on our way for our first ride together.

Spring was breaking everywhere, wild flowers grew in abundance along the roadsides. The air smelt fresh with the scents of tiny mountain roses, heather, and gorse. The forests smelt strongly of eucalyptus and the rising sap of the pines. The three of us set out along a grassy track bordered by wild flowers, which attracted the new season's bees and butterflies.

We came upon an abandoned village, "Is it really totally abandoned Pedro?" I whispered through the silence.

"Yes, the last old man moved out about two years ago."

"I'd like to look inside some of the houses, do you think we can?" I asked.

"Of course," he said dismounting, "we can tie the horses to those trees over there." After tying the horses, I tried the handle of a door on the first stone cottage. "It's open," I said as I peered inside. A feeling of sadness overcame me as we entered. Old dusty furniture had been left behind, too riddled with woodworm to be of any use. These little cottages had once housed families; now they stood alone, neglected, waiting for time, and the elements, to slowly return them to the earth.

"Why did all the people move out Pedro?"

"It probably happened over a period of time," he replied. "You have seen the amount of eucalyptus forests around here, I would say they are the main cause of the decline in mountain village life."

"Eucalyptus trees, how come?" I asked puzzled.

"The trees put down long tap roots, drawing precious water from the earth," he explained. "When you have acres upon acres of these forests, raping the land of its water, the water table cannot cope, the trees drain it and the land becomes barren. These people would have had no choice as their water sources dried up; it became impossible for them to work their land."

The house was cold and damp, the roof leaked, rotting the floorboards. "Once the roof falls in, it doesn't take long for the rain to wash out the mud walls, then the whole house will crumble," he added. Sarah shivered; "Let's go back outside into the sunshine, its freezing in here."

"Yes, we had better be heading back," I shuddered; feeling a bit morose, it was sad to think of all the history held in these skeletons of homes.

As we mounted the horses, Pedro told us of another deserted village that had just been bought by some Germans.

"They bought the whole village for hardly anything, they want to turn it into a holiday village for foreigners, they must be crazy," he laughed.

"Actually, I think it sounds like a really good idea," said Sarah. I agreed with her.

"Northern Europeans would love to be able to experience life in a mountain village in Portugal. I think they could make a success of it, but they will need a lot of money."

" Well, they're German; they've all got money haven't they?" He quipped.

"It's funny you should say that Pedro," I groused, as we wound our way uphill through the forest, the horses carefully tackling the narrow track. "Because I have been noticing that you Portuguese seem to be under the mistaken opinion that all of us foreigners are loaded!"

"Well, it's true, isn't it? You are." he joked cheekily.

"Every time we show an interest in buying a house or land, the price seems to double or even treble overnight." I grumbled, "It's not fair, we're not rich, you probably have more money than us." I couldn't make him change his views, as far as he was concerned, all foreigners were rich.

I was so intent with airing my views, whilst at the same time keeping an eye on the narrow track that we were precariously riding along, that I hadn't noticed the huge mountain now looming over us. I recognized it by its craggy peaks. It was the same mountain I had climbed on Christmas day with my family, when I had fallen into the icy water!

"What's the name of this mountain Pedro? It is so beautiful"

"Yes it is; it's called Peneda de Góis, there are rare ground orchids and other wild flowers that only grow on its slopes and crags. Also beautiful walking tracks: You should explore sometime you will love it. On a clear day you can see all the way to Coimbra. I wouldn't advise that you ride the horses up there though!" he jested.

"I've already explored some of the terrain and fallen in an extremely cold stream," I groaned.

"Oh well, maybe it's best to wait till summertime then" he laughed.

We rode in its shadow for a time, before the track swung around, heading back towards Góis. We had found another beautiful ride, I was beginning to realize that we could ride all day, all week, and not pass the same point twice, there were so many different routes to take, the possibilities for offering riding holidays were endless. The only problem was, we couldn't find a house!

CHAPTER 7

OUR HOUSE

I thought I detected a certain chemistry between Sarah and Pedro. She was due to   return to England shortly, I was going to miss her company, maybe, just maybe, if she formed a relationship with Pedro, she would stay! I hatched a cunning plan, inviting them both to a little party in our field. Paul was also returning to England shortly; he had integrated well and had many friends, his Portuguese language was much better than mine. I was sure he would be back after the summer

He and Craig built a big bonfire, we all sat round it on the ground eating home made beans in tomato sauce, with sausages all cooked over the fire, I had invited a few other people (not wanting it to appear too obvious,) It was a really nice, simple evening; the moon was full, giving a wonderful luminescent glow, Sarah and Pedro were sitting close, talking. Would my plan work?

Later when I glanced over to them, they had disappeared. I never did find out what happened that night, but Sarah returned to England, and a little later, Pedro left Portugal to live with her in England, so part of my plan worked out, but not to my advantage. Something else came out of that night; I was sitting around the fire, talking to one of our new friends called Adam, he was a tall lanky young man of about 28 years, with striking blue eyes; he had a positive energy about him that Steve and I both liked. He said he had a plot of land that he didn't use, and he would be happy for us to grow a crop of oats or maize for the horses. It was a nice offer; he said he would come around the next day, and take us to have a look.

Next day, true to his word Adam arrived on his motorbike, we followed him along a country lane in our car. "I remember this road," said Steve, "we rode along here with the horses and bikes that day, do you remember?"

"Yes," I answered, "It leads to that lovely house by the river." Adam's motorbike slowed down ahead of us. "Steve, he's stopping at the house…our house; the one we've dreamed about." There it stood alone; the nearest neighbour was at least 300 metres away. There were two huge olive trees in the yard, probably planted when the house was built. There was a big orange tree covered in fruit and two old hawthorn trees. The house was built from river boulders and mud. It looked as though it had been plastered at some point, but most of the plaster had disintegrated leaving the boulders exposed. I could clearly hear the river rushing below.

"This is my house," said Adam, "It was a ruin when I bought it three years ago, the end wall had collapsed, and the roof was sagging. I have built up the wall and repaired the roof. That's all I've had time to do." We walked up a set of stone steps covered in moss, that were worn in the middle from centuries of use. Adam opened a big heavy old door. "Be careful where you tread, the floor's rotten in places." We made our way into the centre of a large room, there were holes knocked out for windows, but no frames or glass in them. It was more like a building site inside, with roof tiles and wood piled up against the walls, which had a rough grey render mix on them, but had not been painted.

It was just like a draughty old barn inside, except for one thing. The roof! It was quite exceptional. When you entered the house, your eyes were automatically drawn upwards. Adam re-used most of the ancient chestnut beams. All they had needed was a clean to remove the surface woodworm. The wood was so old and hard even the woodworm had not been able to burrow through. The main room was 5 metres x 10 metres. There were two huge beams running across the width of the room, and an equally long one along the ridge which was 6 metres high. He had planked the whole roof in new pine leaving the rafters exposed running at 18 inches apart. The effect of the new pine against the ancient almost black chestnut, was very eye catching. He rescued and cleaned by hand most of the old tiles, and always kept an eye out for old ruins where there may be some undamaged tiles of the same type that he could salvage, as this type of tile was not sold any more.

Apart from the dramatic roof, the room was rather uninviting, with rotting floorboards that had given way in places. It was cold and damp even on a warm spring day. There were no stairs; so we had to go back down the outside steps and through another old heavy door, to enter two more large rooms, with no windows just ventilation slits, and earthen floors. They would have housed animals in the past. Adam reckoned the house was more than 200 years old. In those times people often slept above their animals, welcoming the warmth that radiated up through the wooden floor....but what about the smell?

There was another little room, which had been the original kitchen. In the old days, people cooked over an open fire, which was in the corner of the room, some smoke escaped through the tiles; the roof would not have been boarded in those days, but still the room would have been constantly smoky. The walls had been black. Adam told us he had scraped off all the black from the walls, re-rendered, and painted the little room with whitewash. In his wood shed he had some beautiful old medronheiro trunks. Medronheiro (strawberry tree) is a very hard spiraling wood; with the bark removed and the wood polished it made a perfect frame for a four poster bed which he hoped would impress his girlfriend. I was sure she would be impressed; we certainly were. It was a charming little room; the only habitable room in the house.

Outside made up for the drab interior, beautiful woodland surrounded the house. There were ancient Sobreiros which are cork oak trees, also medronheiros, pine, eucalyptus, mimosa, and a wealth of undergrowth; heather, gorse, and ferns, all pinpricked by tiny flowering wild iris, hyacinth and rock roses. The river was just 50 metres below us. I could see it clearly, cascading over boulders. We all walked down a narrow path to the river, which was dammed to control the flow by a series of weirs about every half-mile. One of these weirs was just below the house; the water tumbled noisily over it before meandering on its way.

Bordering the river was the piece of land that Adam had talked about. It was about half an acre of good fertile soil. No water shortage here! I was imagining what it would be like to live in such an idyllic scene and I'm sure Steve was having similar thoughts, when Adam's voice brought us back from our dreams. "You can do what you like with the land; I won't have time to use it for years." We were all standing looking back up at the house, it was south facing, standing in complete sun. "Would you sell it?" Steve asked impulsively.

"No," answered Adam, "I'm going back to England to try to persuade my girlfriend to come and live here and make babies."

"It's a great house," said Steve wistfully.

"Yeah," answered Adam. " I'm going for a swim," he said, stripping off and diving into the water.

"Thanks for the use of the land, we might put some corn in," Steve called as Adam surfaced from his dive. "Have a good time in England, we'll see you when you come back."

We both waved to our new friend as we walked a little way along the river bank, gazing up at the house. We were brought back to reality by the sound of splashing from the river. We both turned to see two big otters repeatedly rearing up out of the water, fighting, like a pair of sparring kangaroos! They were totally oblivious of us, too taken up in their struggle for supremacy. We just stood there dumbfounded for about five minutes, before one of the otters dived down and swam off defeated. I know they are very territorial, so they were probably two males fighting over territory; but spectacular to watch!

We walked back up the track to our car, amazed by what we had just witnessed but still in low spirits. It was the house of our dreams, even more so now; but dreams don't always come true and we must accept that and carry on with our search.

During the next month, we had a couple of meetings with Roberto from the council. We had been living in the field with the horses for over 3 months now. In this time we had come to realize that the road, which the land and little house backed onto, was quite well used, especially by the big trucks taking the logged eucalyptus to the factories. Whenever a truck passed by, the little house shook right down to its foundations. "Maybe it's not the ideal setting to live," said Steve one day, as another truck rumbled past. I was inclined to agree with him. It had seemed so perfect at first, but we would have to put a lot of money into renovating a house that would never be ours, and have the annoyance of big trucks rumbling past our door.

We had now found out that we could not have a contract as the land was common land; it had been gifted to the council for agricultural or grazing use. Roberto thought that a riding school would be allowed within this parameter but the plans had been sent to a higher office in Lisbon. We would just have to wait.

The horses were very happy and settled in their new home, it was ideal for them, but we were getting fed up with living in the caravan. We needed a home.

One evening there was a knock on the caravan door. "Adam, how nice to see you, come in." I offered him a glass of wine, and we all sat down. "How was England," asked Steve.

"Not so good," answered Adam, looking thoughtful. "I've come to ask you if you still want to buy my house?" The room fell silent. "Yes" we both said together, my heart was soaring! "Why," I added, "what went wrong?"

"My girlfriend doesn't want to leave England to live here," he said sadly, "and I've decided that the house is too big a project to keep as a holiday home. I would spend all my holidays working on renovations for the next 20 years."

We agreed with him. The house was a full time job, but Steve had experience in building, and carpentry: we could do it. The house had the potential to be lovely, but it was the location we were paying for. We agreed a price. "You can move in whenever you like, we can sort out the paper work later." Adam shrugged, handing over the keys there and then. "Be happy." With that he left us. We were the new owners of the most beautiful spot in Portugal.

A letter arrived at Quinta da Ribeira a few days later, addressed to
The mad English people with horses.
Góis
Portugal

I laughed as I read the address aloud to Steve. "Who can this be from and how did the postman know to deliver it to us; do we look mad?" It was from Steve and Carrie who we had visited in France. They were very cross because we hadn't contacted them to give an address or let them know what was happening. I went to the local cafe and gave them a ring explaining that we hadn't really had an address until now, and in fact we hadn't even moved in yet. I told them a little about our new house, and they said they wanted to come and visit. Although I wanted to see them, the house was not suitable to live in, and wouldn't be for a while. We would still be living in the caravan, I tried to stall them, but they were adamant, they were leaving France and driving to Portugal in the next few days.

We hitched up the caravan, and drove the three kilometers to our new house. We parked it in the garden, under an olive tree, where it stood for many years. The horses were to stay in the fields at Quinta da Ribeira which meant I would have to travel the three kilometres twice a day to care for them, but I didn't mind, I was so excited about our move and to be restoring our lovely old house.

Four days later, our friends arrived with their two boys Jamie and Robbie who were a similar age to Craig. It was lovely for him to see his old playmates, they spent most of the week by the river, fishing, swimming and making camps in the forest. We had only one safe room, the little bedroom with the four poster bed. All four of them had to sleep in there together. We were still sleeping in our caravan, luckily the weather was kind to us; we lived mainly outdoors, lighting a fire in the yard every evening, and sitting around eating our meal and drinking too much delicious French wine that they had brought with them.

A little Portuguese peasant farmer had been tending his field below our house. He walked slowly past us as we sat outside in the early evening, celebrating with a bottle of expensive Bordeaux that Carrie had bought as a special treat to mark the occasion. Steve asked him to join us for a drink. This was obviously what the little farmer had hoped for. He readily took the glass from Steve, and downed the whole glass in one go! Carrie's face took on a look of horror, as the farmer held his glass out for a refill, and downed the second glass as quickly as the first. She gave Steve a warning look, muttering through clenched teeth, "Don't you dare refill his glass again, he didn't even taste it. It never touched the sides!" With the bottle drained, the little man took his leave. Carrie has never forgiven Steve to this day. We had some good days out with our friends, we climbed to the top of our nearest mountain, which was easy going to start with, but the top was quite difficult...for me anyway. The three boys had a great time, leaping ravines and scrambling up to the craggy peak, with me stumbling along behind!

Something we had wanted to do for a while was to explore the Palace of Buçaco, which started life in the 17th century as a convent. It is an ornate building with Manueline facades, and baroque altarpieces, and some of the most intricate azulejos I had seen. But the gardens were what we had come to see. The monks had travelled the world during the 17th century and brought back cuttings and saplings of a vast amount of different trees, which they planted in the gardens of Buçaco. The majority are still there today, it is a wonderful garden where peacocks roam free. The Palace is now a prestigious hotel, I spoke to an American who was staying there, she said it had a 'dilapidated charm of past elegant grandeur', which she loved; preferring it to the more modern style of hotel that she was used to.

I took Carrie out riding, I was always looking for new tracks, which meant I often got lost. I had found it helpful to tie pieces of blue binder twine which came from the hay bales, onto branches of trees as I rode along. On this instance, it was getting dark and I was a little worried about finding the track that led home, when 'hey presto' there was a flash of blue hanging from a branch. We searched around and found another, then I recognised where we were, not far from home at all.

We swam every day in the river, it was still only early June and the water was cold, leaving your body feeling tingly and alive! We had seen kingfishers flying at great speed just above the water many times, but this particular week, we were seeing them every day, and they seemed much too tame, their flying abilities were ungainly and desperate. They would perch on a reed, and just watch us, usually two or three of them. It dawned on us that they were young, and had just left their nest further upstream, their parents were still feeding them; they hadn't refined their flying methods yet, nor could they catch their own fish, but as the week wore on, their confidence had grown and we watched them leave to find their own territory; one by one. I missed their beauty, yet I felt that I had been privileged to glimpse into the life of a wild creature. A couple of weeks later, Steve, Craig and I were sitting on the veranda, just watching the river flowing beneath us, when we became aware of animals playing on the opposite bank and diving into the water. It was otters; we sat there spellbound for minutes, watching three of them gambolling up a bank, around a tree, then diving back into the water. We were enchanted; none of us even thought to get a camera, we just enjoyed the moment.

Sam and Jacky asked us if we would like to go for a day out in Coimbra, which was about 45 kilometres to the west. Coimbra to us mountain folk was a real big city! It even had a cinema! We were to go in their car to the nearest train station which was in a village called Serpins; about 15 minutes from our house. From there we could catch a lovely little mountain train, that slowly trundled through the scenic countryside and came to a halt in the centre of Coimbra. We had used this train before, it was an enjoyable journey and much more relaxing than driving into a busy city.

Sam and Jacky picked the three of us up in their car, and we had just arrived at Serpins station, when Jacky, a confirmed cat lover, shouted. "Stop! Stop Sam, that looks like a little kitten in the middle of the road."

Sam screeched to a halt, and sure enough, looking up at us with huge blue eyes, was a cowering scrap of ginger. Jacky, who had two cats already, jumped out and picked up the kitten. She started to question a group of men standing idle outside a café. They all just shrugged. They didn't know where it had come from. Hopefully Jacky made them feel a little ashamed, but I doubted it. There were so many stray animals around in those days, that life was cheap.

Jacky was furious, she asked in the bar, and in the shop next door, but nobody wanted to help her. She tucked the kitten inside her coat, and mustering up as much stiff upper lip as possible, climbed back into the car. I could see from the look on Sam's face that he had already resigned himself to giving up his day in Coimbra and becoming nursemaid, but Jacky came up with the idea to take him to another friend who lived nearby. "She could look after him today and we could pick him up tonight," she cooed, happily snuggling the needy, soft ginger kitten under her chin. Jacky's friend Tess was more than happy to be nursemaid for the day and we just managed to catch the next train into Coimbra.

It seemed strange to be amongst bustling crowds again, but we all enjoyed ourselves, shopping and eating Chinese food, but the highlight of the day was the cinema! We returned late to Jacky's friend, and found her desperately trying to feed the kitten with an eyedropper. "He's struggling to lap, he's too young," she said, looking at us with concern.

One of Jacky's cats had just finished weaning her young. "I wonder, if the kitten suckled Tara, her milk flow would return?" said Jacky hopefully, "It's worth a try."

It worked, Tara nursed the kitten for a couple of weeks, then Jacky, thinking Tara was suffering from this greedy little cuckoo, presented him to Craig as a gift. He was delighted; I shall never forget the look on his face. A kitten of his very own, he carried him around with him wherever he went, it slept on his head or cuddled up into his neck!

Toby the dog had always hated cats, he looked down his long snout at this intrusion, but the little kitten, not realizing he was supposed to be afraid, would snuggle up to him for warmth. Toby looked at me indignantly; as he would if I had placed a pork chop under his nose and told him not to touch it!

Craig came home from school every day with a new name for his pet. So far it had been called Ginger, Lucky, Tigger, The Lion King, and British Bulldog, (BB). When we took the kitten to the vet for his injections, he put Craig on the spot. "What is his name?" asked the vet,

Craig looked at me for help, "It's your cat, you decide," was all I offered. "British Bulldog," he said proudly. The vet looked amused, but wrote down his name. It was a good name, it suited him, he was very bandy, and a real little fighter.

I can quite assure you that BB often stood for names unprintable! He grew into the most terrible little thief. One day I remember, I came home from the shops, fully loaded. I opened the boot, and carried in six, one litre cartons of milk, putting them on the table, I went back out to the car to get some more shopping. I was only gone for a minute, but in that time, he had jumped up onto the table, punctured with his sharp little teeth, not one, but two cartons of milk, and was greedily lapping the liquid as it dribbled down the carton. On hearing me entering the house, he jumped down in a flash, knowing he had done wrong, and streaked past me down the steps. While I was cleaning up the mess, he had jumped into the boot, ripped open a bag of dog food, and was happily crunching the spilled biscuits!

Another time, I remember, Sam coming to visit and bringing donuts to eat. We were eating ours, but he was busy talking, leaving his unguarded cake on the table. A blur of ginger appeared, grabbed the donut in his mouth, and disappeared through the door, before any of us could move. The donutless Sam made a vain attempt to chase the cat, but he had vanished.

Now you may be wondering if we ever fed this cat. I can quite assure you that we did. He even stole food from poor Toby's bowl, he pushed himself between Toby's front legs, and whilst Toby snarled and showed his fangs in warning, BB nonchalantly crunched his food, totally ignoring him. We have had quite a few cats since, but I have never known another like him. He grew into a big fat lazy cat, Craig would pick him up under his front legs and he would just hang there totally unfazed and too lazy to do anything about it!

Our Portuguese neighbour told us his dog had just had puppies, but he would have to kill them all because he had no homes for them. Mella, who was over for the summer, was horrified. "He can't kill them all, it's not fair on the mother," she cried. "Why don't we have one?" I remembered the last time I had tried to argue with Mella over a dog: She was about 9 or 10 years old, and had become bored watching her father play in a Sunday football match. She had wandered over to the Brighton RSPCA kennels nearby. It had been love at first sight for her, there, sat in his kennel with enormous ears, and a tiny skinny body, was a little black puppy. Mella crouched down and stayed with him for a while, talking softly through the bars to him. She asked the lady on duty what would happen to him, and was told that he would stay in the kennels for a week or so, because he had been taken away from his previous home in such bad condition, then they would try to find a new home for him.

When she came home, she begged and begged and begged, and I said "No! No! No!" Maybe she could sense that my No's, were getting weaker, and after three or four days of non-stop begging I gave in. The RSPCA visited our home to check that we were suitable. I must say they were very thorough, you would have thought we were taking on the supreme champion of Crufts, not a skinny little mongrel.

A few days later, we went to pick him up. This was the first time I had seen him, and had assumed that she would have chosen a pretty little puppy dog; I was quite taken aback when they brought him out to us. As a result of malnutrition, he had a potbelly, but he was so skinny, his backbone was clearly visible, outsized floppy ears crowned his tiny domed head. I suppose beauty is in the eye of the beholder, Mella and Paul were both thrilled with him; he soon lost his nerves, and Toby was a much-loved member of our family for the next fourteen years.

Now I was confronting Mella again. "Oh, come on mum, just a little puppy, Toby would love it, let's just go and have a look." Having a look turned out to be the most fatal thing, we couldn't choose which one to have, so we ended up taking two! Bica and Boneca were such timewasters. Delightful bundles of brown fluff with little black noses and paws. I would hold one in each arm and they would snuffle into my neck making little grunting noises in my ear. I could have hugged them to death.

Word soon spread: soon after, an old woman in a black shawl shouted out to me from the bottom of our steps. She had a basket on her arm, and I thought she had some eggs or something to sell, but as she pulled back the lid, two little faces peered up at me. "Nobody wants them, I will have to kill them," she said, words I seemed to have heard before! "You will never have any rats or mice if you take them, their mother is the best mouser in the village." Actually I had noticed a few mice, in the barn at the horses field, so I agreed to take them. "Put some butter on their paws, and they won't run away," she muttered as she quickly hurried back up the drive, no doubt afraid that I may change my mind.

We called them Batman and Robin. Batman was black and white, with a little black mask around his eyes and nose, Robin, was mainly white with orange splodges. He had a tiny little face and very round eyes, he reminded me of a china doll. I would gladly have carried on taking in waifs and strays, but Steve now called a halt. "No more animals," he said decisively, and I had to agree…for the moment! He was always threatening to make a pair of matching fluffy slippers out of Bica and Boneca, but he loved them all just as much as I did. Boneca and BB were always fighting for the rights to his lap.

Bica loved swimming in our river; she took to it at about 10 weeks old, and after her initial shock of the ground disappearing, she swam with us every day throughout the summer. She used to clamber up on Craig's boogie board, and ride the rapids of our weir. Boneca and Robin would stand on the weir, barking and meowing respectively. When Batman and Robin were old enough, we took them to Quinta da Ribeira, to live with the horses; where they settled in very quickly amongst all the mice!

Whilst Craig, Mella and I had fun with all the animals, Steve was working on renovations to the house. He repaired the floor in the living area, and put in windows, he built a large work surface, with a shelf above, at head height, and a shelf below, to give us more storage. This was to be our kitchen area until we got around to building our eventual kitchen in one of the earthen-floored downstairs rooms. We moved the full-sized gas stove, which we had in the caravan, into the house. Pots, pans, and crockery, were stored underneath the work surface, whilst foodstuff was stored on the shelf above, away from the notorious BB we hoped.

We had no running water, only our little spring, about 20 metres from the house. During the summer the spring ran very slowly, it took about twenty minutes to fill a bucket, so it was a continuous cycle; fetching the full bucket up to the house, and placing an empty one under the spring. Everybody here in the mountains used bottled gas. We cooked by it and had a gas lamp for lighting. We had no electricity, or piped water or a toilet. We had stepped back in time about 100 years.

Steve set about making a toilette extraordinaire. He built a little outdoor wooden chalet, complete with tiled roof and net curtains (no glass). The actual toilet was still just a large hole in the ground, but he built up a box, with a proper toilet seat, so you could actually sit down – such luxury! The interior was decorated with all the postcards we received from friends and well-wishers from all over the world. I added plants and magazines – the feminine touch. Everyone who came to visit wanted a photo of our loo. Some even had themselves featured in it!

We were not missing the TV, but we were missing our music. We had an old car radio which Steve fitted up to a car battery which were both placed on a chair in the main upstairs room. The only music we could play was Portuguese radio, which played more adverts than music. On every hour, after the news, the radio station would play 10 American/English pop songs without any interruption. This was a huge highlight for us, and we would time our coffee breaks to coincide.

Our horses' electric fence also ran on a car battery. Both batteries had to be re-charged every couple of weeks. The local garage, where I was already well known, used to charge us the equivalent of about 30 cents to charge up our batteries. The reason that I was well known at the garage, was because one morning I had noticed a hole in my exhaust pipe, and called in to ask if they could fix it. I had looked up the words for hole and exhaust, so I told the mechanic quite confidently that I had a baraco in my exhaust. The poor man looked completely confused, he relayed my sentence to the rest of the mechanics, then the whole place erupted into laughter at my expense! A young lad working there who spoke a little English, tried to explain the joke to me. Baraco is a type of old shed or shack. Buraco, is a hole! How will I ever live that down.

"What's to be the next project?" I asked Steve, one hot summer's day. "Well, we need a kitchen, but we can manage as we are for a while, we need a bedroom and a bathroom"... "What about a veranda?" I said. Our life was based so much out of doors at that time, it seemed the most important feature. Steve agreed "Who needs kitchens, bedrooms, bathrooms, when you have a veranda"? He was really looking forward to the challenge. Nuno, a young Portuguese man from a nearby village was looking for work, he had taken to popping in for a 'copo de vinho' quite regularly, I had the feeling that he was looking for a chance to get to know Mella better, so he was happy to help. Steve and Nuno took measurements. The veranda was to be the whole length of the house which was 11 metres, and about 2.5 metres wide. We would need upright posts and handrails, joists to go into the wall and of course floorboards. Nuno offered to order them for us from his phone at home as we had no phone line to our house.

About a week later he and Steve set out in the horsebox, to pick up the materials from Eduardo at the wood yard in Arganil. They passed through an old village and noticed a house with the roof gone and the walls falling down – a ruin. They could see inside, from the high seats of the truck, and Steve noticed a huge chestnut beam, which looked just about the right size to support half of our veranda. They stopped to investigate. You couldn't even buy a piece of wood like that in England these days, thought Steve. It was seven metres long, and nearly 30 cm thick. Two old men were sitting on a wall nearby, Nuno went to talk to them about the beam, he shouted over to Steve, "Podes levar por dois contos." (You can take it for the equivalent of 8 pounds.) Steve couldn't believe his luck; he was always on the lookout for good old hard wood, it's much better than new, he always said.

Steve and Nuno couldn't even lift it; Nuno seemed to be related to the whole of the Góis area. Luckily his brother lived just up the road and he and a friend had just arrived home for lunch; they were only too happy to come and help. Of course, this meant Steve had to go and sample their wine, but his digestion was hardening up by now, through necessity! This wine he genuinely enjoyed, and asked if he could buy some. Nuno's brother said, if Steve brought some 5 litre empty bottles, he would fill them up for us for 2 euros each!

Nothing could be done in a hurry in Portugal; even a small job would take all day. Going to the wood yard to buy materials, I had expected to take about an hour. Steve and Nuno had left at about 10am. They returned at 4.30pm. Steve explained that by the time they finally reached the wood yard, after finding and loading the chestnut beam it had closed for a 2 hour lunch break; so they went to visit some other relatives of Nuno and had joined in their lunch, of fresh barbecued sardines, bread, and of course more wine! If I had been annoyed, I soon forgot it when I saw the beautiful chestnut beam. "It would take me a week's wages to buy something like that in England." Steve said, delighted with his purchase.

The beam would span half the veranda. We already had the other beam, the old boy who drank half a bottle of Carrie's Bordeaux had said we could cut a eucalyptus tree from his land. Steve had chopped and milled it himself with a chainsaw. He built a central concrete column; one day we will find the time to stone face it, so that it blends in with the rest of the house.

There had obviously been a veranda at some time in the past. The original outer walls were still in reasonable condition; Steve only had to re-build the tops of each end wall. The two big beams were to sit on the end walls, and meet on the concrete pillar in the middle. This was to prove a very dodgy operation. The veranda was 11 metres long, and we needed to lift these 2 huge beams, 3 metres up into the air: we called in a posse of willing hands, Nuno brought along a couple of his friends, and Mella, Sam and Jacky were all there to help us lift the two beams into place. The chestnut beam was slightly banana shaped, we erected a scaffold and lifted the beam into position, it sat very precariously. When we lifted the eucalyptus beam up onto the central column, it touched the end of the chestnut banana beam, and caused it to swing violently from side to side three metres up in the air! Steve was directing from underneath it, four strong men were standing on a scaffold; they grabbed hold of it and with all their strength, managed to stabilize it into position...Phew.

It was a close shave for Steve, who had been frantically trying to calculate which way it would fall and which way he should run. He looked like a chicken with its head chopped off, and we all burst into a nervous laughter of relief. We paid our friends with a delicious barbecue and plenty of our newly acquired wine.

We were offered some old oak beams that had been burnt in a fire. Steve scraped all the old burnt wood off from the surface; underneath the wood was still good and hard. We would position them each side of the concrete column to form the skeleton of our new veranda.

When you are working on an old house, nothing is simple. The next step was to attach floor joists, which in Portugal are called barrotes. They would span from the wall of the house onto the two newly erected beams. The house is made of river boulders of various sizes packed together with mud. The walls are at least 80 cm. thick. Steve wanted to have joists every 45cm. This meant he had to dig out many of the boulders, some huge, so that the joists could be inserted into the wall and cemented in.

If a really big boulder had to come out, he would rebuild around the joist with cement and smaller rocks. Sometimes, he would mix up some cement to fill in what looked like a small hole, and hear the cement thud to the bottom some way below. He began to realize that our house was a maze of mice runs. It would have been a lovely city for them, but for us it was a danger sign. With the mud gone, the house could crumble. Whenever Steve heard the long thud, he would fill the hole up completely with small boulders and cement to reinforce it. I only hoped the inhabitants were out that day! It was a long laborious job, as everything had to be done by hand, because we had no electricity to run tools to speed things up.

The end wall which Steve had re-built was about 30 cm. thick. When he had completed enough joists, for me to reach the wall from the veranda door, I would precariously step from one joist to the next, with a 3 metre drop below me, until I reached the outer wall. I was also carrying a glass of wine and a nice comfy cushion to perch on. The wall, was just about wide enough to accommodate my bottom, so at last I could sit and look out over my new home, watch the shadows glide silently across the mountain as the sun went down, see the changing colours of the evening sky, and welcome the first stars that brought with them the lovely cool night air. I looked down at the river with the white water gushing over the weir. The sound of the water is always audible. In winter it is a torrent of angry sound, in summer it is a mellow gentle lullaby. Sometimes when I closed my eyes, I thought I could hear children's laughter bubbling up into the air; the happy gurgling of the river as it journeyed endlessly onward. I felt very strongly that the aura of this lovely old house would always be within me.

CHAPTER 8

CIGANO & SILVER MOON

We started to get a few enquiries for riding lessons. One was from a children's charity that brought 100 inner city children for 2 week holidays; hiking in the mountains and swimming in the rivers. The charity wanted the children, who were all from very poor backgrounds, to experience horse riding, which they would never get a chance to do in Lisbon. The children visited us on a rota whereby ten children came for a two hour session, then the following day the charity brought another ten children. This was repeated every day for 2 weeks, when all the children returned to Lisbon. They were then replaced by another 100 very excited children. Roxy soon proved that he was not suitable for children, barging, nipping and even threatening to kick the unsuspecting children thronging around. He was removed in disgrace to his stable and the work fell to Guv and Smartie.

It was hard work for us as well as the horses, but the children loved it. They all helped to groom them and had lots of fun trying to put on the saddles and bridles. There was always much excitement, at first some of the children were afraid, but Guv and Smartie always won them over. Once the saddles and bridles were on, the children took turns to ride the horses around the newly completed (yes tractor man did eventually turn up!) sand school. Afterwards, with one child leading the horse and another riding, we set off for a ride around the field. Craig walked beside Smartie just in case there were any problems, and I walked beside Guv.

Once everybody had ridden, we took off the saddles and bridles, the children loved to see the horses rolling in the sand, which they always did after being ridden. Lastly the children showered the horses with the soap and a hose. This was always great fun; and of course it wasn't only the horses that got a soaking. On one of our early sessions, I showed the children how to spray some soap onto the horses backs, but got my words in a muddle. I told the children to spray some sopa (soup) onto the horses backs! Of course, all the children thought this was very funny, I was laughing too, having a picture in my mind of spraying the horses with tomato soup! Craig enjoyed helping me with these sessions, it was a chance for him to meet Portuguese children, and sometimes the leaders of the group would invite him to go swimming with them afterwards in the river.

I have not mentioned yet that the summer holidays were three months long. At the end of the summer term we visited Craig's teacher. She told us that although he had settled in very well, and seemed to understand what was being said to him, he would not talk. At first she had thought him shy, but now she was becoming worried by it. Her thoughts were that he was a perfectionist, if he didn't know one word in a sentence, he would not say the whole sentence. It was vital for him to mix with Portuguese people during the long holidays. The locals living around our house were mainly older generation, they were all very kind to him. Our nearest neighbour who lived about 300 metres from us, was a lovely friendly lady called Maria, whom we used to buy eggs from, she always had a little cake or some biscuits for Craig. One day I sent him along to her with an empty cardboard egg box to buy some eggs, and he came back with a live chicken, hanging by a piece of string, tied to its feet! "Maria said it's about time we had our own chickens, she has some more to sell if you want them, but this one is mine," he said proudly, clutching the string. The poor bird's head was dangling about five centimetres from the road.

"What are we going to do with a chicken?" I asked dumbfounded. "We have nowhere to put it." "You're not going to eat it," said Craig defensively.

"No of course not, she will have to live in with the dogs," I said.

"Take her in there now, and get that string off the poor things legs." Bica and Boneca slept in a little room under our bedroom, along with all Steve's tools. "Maria said all she needed was a perch," Craig added as he carefully untied the string, "I think I will call her Freaky," he said.

From the squawking and flapping of wings coming from inside the room, that was a very apt name. Craig went off to cut a perch for her from our overgrown olive tree in the yard. "What do chickens eat?" I asked ignorantly,

"Maria said she will eat anything, but she loves worms, I will go and dig her some in a minute."

After a couple of days, we let her out, to run around the yard, she was very tame, and would come running when you called her name. She was no trouble, she used to put herself to bed at night, "Maybe we should have some more," I said to Steve one morning, "after all one chicken won't lay enough eggs for us all." "Well okay, but they are not pets, they are to provide us with eggs, and if they don't; we will eat them, agreed?"

"Yes okay." I answered; not at all sure I could eat one of my own animals. We went to visit Maria, and came back with Fanny and Frannie. We shut them in for a couple of days, handling them a lot to tame them as we had done with Freaky, then they were allowed out in the yard. All the animals made the house look like a proper farmyard. I had always lived in suburbia, for me, this was a dream slowly unfolding. We didn't have much land around the house but either side of us were just ruins and forest land, so we had no neighbours for our animals to annoy.

Steve envisaged planting an orchard in our field below the house; the same field that Adam had offered us to grow maize in. Now it belonged to us, trees were a better option. Water was no problem down there by the river, so he planned to plant lots of different varieties of fruit and nut trees. Peaches and nectarines grow well here in the warmer climate, as do figs, oranges and lemons, tangerines, walnuts and a fruit not common in England: diospiros (persimmon) These look like a large tomato. The trees lose all their leaves in wintertime, and the fruits hang, large, orange and bulbous on the bare branches. When we saw them in the shops, we had to try some, so picking out a couple of nice firm looking fruits, we took them home. When we bit into them we nearly turned our mouths inside out, they were horrible, acrid and bitter. Well, we thought, the Portuguese can keep them!

When we told one of the local ladies what we thought of this strange fruit, she clapped her hands and laughed in glee at our ignorance. She explained that you have to wait until they resemble a rotten tomato, really squishy, before attempting to eat them. " Here, try this one" she said. It looked like an exploded cricket ball! As she carefully placed it in a dish, its innards oozed out. "Try it, you will like it" she beckoned. Not wishing to appear rude, we tentatively sampled the unappetizing gunk in front of us. It was surprisingly delicious. She told us that they were full of vitamins, and an important part of Portuguese winter diet. They have since become one of our favorite fruits and these days you can buy non astringent varieties all year round.

The children's riding groups didn't pay us much money, but helped with Craig's language problems immensely. He was quite knowledgeable about horses, and of course the children were full of questions. It gave him a feeling of importance, it was a subject he knew more about than them. If he could not think of the right word to use, they would all try to guess it for him, and it became a bit of a game. Another person who was very important to Craig at this time was Nuno. He lived locally and had become a family friend. He was so patient; even I attempted to talk to him. He was the same age as Paul, who had now returned to England for the summer, so he became Craig's substitute big brother. He was a very handsome typically Latin looking young man with swarthy skin, black hair and deep brown eyes. Mella and Nuno had been seeing quite a bit of each other over the last month or so, the problem was she couldn't speak Portuguese and he couldn't speak English, so they had to take Craig with them wherever they went to translate for them!

During the summer, now as then, every village holds its own festival. They play awful taped wailing music through tinny crackly loudspeakers, for three days. Usually Friday, Saturday and Sunday. On Saturday, it often goes on all night! Because we live in a valley, and have mountain villages all around us, we are subjected to this din every weekend as each village celebrates their summer festas. That first summer, Nuno took Craig on the back of his motor bike to many festas, where he would meet his school friends in an out of school situation. When Craig returned to school at the end of September, his teacher was happy and amazed at his progress, and when he left her school a year later, she asked us to write a report for her CV, it could be helpful for her future employment to have taught an English boy. We thought she had done a great job.

The two older boys, Carlos and Nuno, whom we had befriended at the Monastery, still visited us to ride the horses and cajole me into learning some verbs. We were having Portuguese lessons once a week with our teacher in Góis but it was slow going. "It's too much of a shock for my old brain cells," I complained, "Trying to kick start them back into learning after nearly 25 years of doing very little. It's not easy!" I remembered my old headmistress standing up and preaching to us all saying, "You are English - you do not need another language." It was her fault that I was having these problems now, we had not even had the chance to learn French at school, because she wouldn't have it.

The day before my birthday, the boys told us that the white stallion, who had stolen a piece of my heart, and lived in the underground stable near the Monastery, was for sale. We took a trip back over to the Monastery to talk to the owner, who was now running the new riding school there, to find out more. "The horse took a bad fall while I was riding him," he said, leading us over to the dark prison.

"I didn't think you ever rode them," I answered.

"I don't very often," he said. "I'm too busy. In my opinion, he will not recover soundness, he's too old."

"How old is he," I asked.

"About 16 years, I think." I was now standing face to face with this beautiful creature. He had a large scar from his neck down almost to his girth, I touched it gently. "Ah, yes that is an old scar. He was a bullfighting horse many years ago; he was gored by a bull and lost his nerve so was sold as a riding horse. You can take him, he is of no use to me," he added.

"What's his name" I asked,

"He doesn't have one, I just call him horse."

How could I leave him there, chained to a wall, I held my hand out to him, but he flinched and turned his head away. His knee was very swollen, but he could put weight on it, Steve and I spoke for a minute, then turning to the owner, Steve said, "We'll pick him up tomorrow, if that's alright with you." Next day, my birthday, we drove him to his last home.

That night, we were standing out on our newly completed veranda, trying to think of a name for him, he must have had a name at some time but we would never find out what it was. The moon rose, silver and full, "Silver Moon," I said. "Thank you darling, he is a wonderful present."

I was so excited at the thought of giving Silver Moon his liberty, he would have a big stable, where he could lay down, and move around, and once he had settled, he could have a field to graze in. It didn't happen like that at all. Every time I entered the stable over the next few weeks, he would shuffle to the back and stand with his head near the wall. He was tense and nervous of my every move. It was almost as if he missed his chains. It was so disappointing; I suppose it was similar to a human prisoner, receiving his freedom after being locked up for a long time. He was institutionalized. He needed time to acclimatize.

Finally the breakthrough came. One morning when I arrived at the stables to feed breakfasts, his lovely old head was over the door, and not only that, he had lain down during the night for the first time; easy to spot the brown stains on his white coat. From that day on his head was always over the door, surveying his domain, he would whinny for breakfast along with the other three horses, but as soon as I pulled the bolt on the stable door, he would still back away from me, but he was becoming more and more relaxed and sure of himself, in my presence.

He had a wonderful mane, long and curly. One fine warm day, I gave him a shower; he enjoyed it. He had obviously been well looked after at some time, his manners were impeccable. After his shower, with his mane brushed out, his coat had taken on a mother of pearl type sheen. I have never seen anything quite like it before. He really was exceptionally beautiful, until you got down to his knees, poor boy, but he didn't seem in too much pain, and his spirits were picking up daily. He loved to nuzzle and smell me, as if I was one of his herd. I had to be careful not to wear perfume. It drove him wild, what he needed was a girlfriend!

We heard of a bi-monthly market in Coimbra called Feira dos 7 e 23, (it was always held on the 7th and 23rd of each month) and that horses and other livestock were sold there. It was on a large flat piece of land on the outskirts of the city, alongside the River Mondego. We had been thinking it might be nice to buy a pony. Guv was very good with children, but he was so big; maybe before next summer, we could buy a pony. We were only going to the market to look, to check out prices and to see the type of horses for sale. We heard lots of squawking and saw many different types of fowl for sale, but no horses.

Ahead of us, on a patch of waste ground I could see what looked like small hooves! I moved closer and realized that there was a pile of goat or sheep hooves that looked as if they had only recently been hacked off..."What the" I started to say, but stopped myself deciding it was best not to know! There were no signs of any goats or sheep; I was relieved that we had arrived a bit late.

Just then my attention was drawn to a single horse, it seemed to be the only one at the market. I paused and ran my eyes over this poor skeleton, standing, tied to a lorry with his head hanging low. "Come on" ushered Steve, "we are supposed to be running a riding centre, not a charity."

Before he could drag me away, a group of gypsies descended on us, obviously they were the owners of the horse. They were all gabbling at once and talking with their hands, trying to get our attention. They mentioned the equivalent sum of two thousand pounds. We both laughed and carried on walking, but by now someone had tacked up the horse, and was mounting. The saddle was a wonderfully ornate Portuguese bullfighting saddle with big box stirrups, to protect your feet from the bull, and a wide ornate leather wall around the front and back of the saddle; I presumed this was also for protection. The man was dressed in black trousers and waistcoat, with a frilly white shirt, and black boots with huge star type spurs.

The scraggy skeleton looked transformed under all this, and as the man mounted we were compelled to watch. He rode around in tight circles, trotting and cantering with the utmost skill, and to add a touch of flamboyance the horse reared on demand.

They kept urging Steve to try him, but Steve was no great master, and this horse did not look anything like the armchair ride he was used to with Guv. I was wearing a flimsy short summer dress, and sandals, but somehow entered into the spirit of all the excitement around us, and decided to try the horse myself. The horse went round and round in circles, making it impossible for me to mount. A gypsy came to hold the horse, and Steve helped me up; the saddle felt wonderful, just like an armchair, but my dress was now up around my thighs! Luckily the leather wall around the front and back of the saddle ensured that my modesty was preserved!

Quite a crowd had gathered to watch the spectacle. I walked the horse off, he seemed quiet enough, we broke into a trot away from the crowd to the far end of the marketplace. I circled the horse in 10 metre circles; he seemed very responsive. I was enjoying the feel of him; he was very springy and had a way of going like a horse from a Clint Eastwood movie, with a high stepping walk from his front legs, but almost trotting with his back legs. I began to reason with my better judgment, we don't really need a pony, and a horse like this would be good for experienced riders, (not that we had any). If the gypsies were desperate to sell, this horse could be bought for a bargain.

I turned him calmly back towards the crowd, my mind full of how I could convince Steve as easily as I had convinced myself! Suddenly, the horse leapt forward, and galloped flat out back towards the crowd; he took me completely by surprise. I pulled hard on the reins; there was no response at all. I tried to circle him, but it was useless. People were now screaming in terror and scattering in all directions. I can remember seeing all these blurs of colour as men, women, and children ran for their lives. I was totally out of control, and we were heading for the main market square where people had stalls selling Reebok trainers, Levi's, plastic dustbins, and pots and pans. I knew some tricks for stopping bolting horses, Roxy had taught me well, and finally as I took one rein shorter than the other, and continually pulled it, released it, pulled it, released it, he began to take heed and slow down to a pace where I could circle him. We stopped about five metres from the first row of stalls. I could see some of the proprietors making the sign of the cross on their chests as they stood there!

Panic stricken, I was totally exhausted, Steve ran up to help me down, and I almost collapsed into his arms, my knees giving out under me. The horse was now standing docile and calm, just as I had first seen him, with his head hanging low. The gypsies were not far behind Steve, and the gawping crowd had followed. When I had regained my posture, I said in my best Portuguese. "No thank you, I don't think he is suitable." We tried to lose ourselves among the stalls, but the gypsies followed us, jabbering constantly. They hadn't done the chain on his bridle up tightly enough, it wouldn't happen again, they were saying. It wouldn't happen again, I knew that nothing would persuade me to get on that suicidal menace again! "No, no, no," we said, " go away."

I glanced again at the horse, standing so quietly. Why had he behaved like that, was it fear, or pain? I had noticed that his mouth was sore. They told us he was 5 years old; I laughed, I had looked at his teeth and aged him at more like 17-20 years. The gypsies played their final card. If he was not sold today, tomorrow he went to the butcher. What could I say? I had bought my first pony at an English auction when I was only 15 years old. I had outbid the slaughter man then, and that pony Bracken, repaid me with 15 years of fun and love.

"Okay, I will try him again." I heard myself say. I mounted and went through a similar routine to before, circling him and trotting up to the end of the market place. But when we turned to come back towards the crowd, I was ready for him; he sensed it and made no attempt to bolt. Everybody clapped and cheered as I dismounted, this time in a more ladylike fashion!

The gypsy took off the saddle and bridle, took the 400 pounds we offered for him, and vanished. They left me with a bit of rope tied around his neck. Steve had to drive back home to pick up the horsebox, so Craig and I waited there for nearly 2 hours with our new horse. We took him to a patch of grass, which he ate hungrily.

A young lad approached us looking intently at the horse. Craig's language was good enough now to understand what he was saying. "Este cavalo é do meu tio, vocês roubaram-no."(This is my uncle's horse; you've stolen it.) Without another word, he ran off leaving us wondering what was going to happen next.

Soon after, we saw a policeman on a motorbike, riding across the almost deserted market place. He stopped in front of us, and started asking questions; he wanted the bill of sale, but we didn't have one. He was very stern, and he had a gun, which scared me. Confronted by police, I always feel guilty, even though I'm usually not! He asked for the name of the person who sold us the horse, but we didn't know. "Ciganos" (gypsies) was all I could say.

I think he sized up the situation, a woman wearing a summer dress, with a young boy; we hardly looked like horse thieves. He nodded to us to stay where we were, and roared off.

He obviously knew where the gypsies camped, because within 20 minutes, he was back, with a bill of sale for us. I thanked him profusely, and he actually smiled at us as he rode off. We were both so relieved when our horsebox turned into the market place. The horse almost ran up the ramp of our lorry, I think he was as glad to be leaving the market place as we were. As we drove off, groups of people standing drinking at the market bar shouted and waved at us. They had obviously enjoyed the show; I bet there was a lot of talk that night in the surrounding bars, of the crazy English woman galloping around their market place wearing hardly any clothes!

The name the gypsies gave the horse was Rei (King) but I wanted to call him Cigano (Gypsy). This would be the first time I had changed a horse's name, Silver was different, he didn't have a name! Would it bring us bad luck, as folklore says?

We took poor Cigano home, and stabled him next to Silver. I planned to give him at least a month's rest, because he had sores around his mouth, and also on his back, where the saddle had not fitted him properly. He was also painfully thin. He needed worming and some good food, I wanted to build a trusting relationship with him so I spent time just being with him, talking to him, trying to break through his barrier. He would stand stock still, staring with empty eyes, as if to say, please go, please leave me alone.

Horses use body language a lot. Roxy for instance had a very talkative body! Sometimes he would smile kindly with his eyes, and sometimes with devilment, he could also be terribly sulky. If he thought I had a tit-bit in my pocket for him, his eyes would light up and his top lip would go to one side. He was the biggest baby in the world when hurt, if he had a cut, and got a whiff of antiseptic cream, he would go into a terrible rage, just like a spoiled child, stamping his feet and pretending to bite.

The difference between the two horses was stark. Cigano truly had a broken spirit, and after a month of kindness, good food and veterinary help (he had a heavy worm burden), I was beginning to doubt if it could ever be repaired.

CHAPTER 9

FRANCISCO

During the summer, we had a few people come riding, not enough to make a living, but it was a start. We had done no advertising, so it was mainly people passing by on the road into Góis, who on seeing the horses grazing in the fields, stopped out of curiosity to enquire. We had been planning to have a sign to advertise the riding school to the public. I was giving lessons to a local girl, who told me she was an artist, and I asked her if she would be interested in making a sign for us in return for riding lessons. Between us we designed a picture of two rearing horses, with the words Escola de Equitação (Riding School) in an arc under the horses' rearing front legs. It looked spectacular on paper.

Steve bought a 3 metre x 3 metre square of plywood, and gave it five coats of sky blue paint for the background. She was to do the painting during her summer vacation. We bought all the paints and brushes that she would need, and looked forward to her starting work. We were so disappointed when she called one day to say that she would not be able to do the painting, as she had to go urgently to Lisbon. We could not afford to pay an artist, so we would just have to abandon the plan.

A week or so later, two young English girls passed by, and noticing our English registered car, they stopped for a chat. They had hitch hiked around Spain and Portugal. Nikki was studying law and Sara was studying art. Sara asked what the blue painted board standing in the corner was for, so we told her of our disappointment. "I'll paint it for you." she said brightly. She had some experience; she had helped revamp a restaurant in London, painting murals freehand on the walls. We had only the sheet of ply to lose, so we agreed. She had five days before they were due to return to England, so she would have to start immediately.

They were great company, telling us many tales of their travels. Paul had returned to England, but the little caravan was still in the horses' field. They jumped at the chance to sleep in it, preferring to stay there, because it was much nearer the town than our house which was three kilometres away. They could walk into town at night and have a bit of fun. "And the barn is a good dry place to paint," added Sara. The caravan had a little stove, "Wow," they exclaimed with joy, "hot food!" We took them to Góis market next morning, and stocked up on food for them. They would accept no money, only food.

One morning when I arrived to feed the horses, there was Nikki, the law student, arguing in English with a poor Portuguese council worker, who was scratching his head looking totally confused! He had come to pick up some old barrels of bitumen from our forecourt. We had been asking for some time to have them removed, so you can imagine his surprise, as Nikki, pen and paper in hand, took down his registration number and adamantly refused to allow him to take them away, thinking that they were our property. I arrived just in time before he drove off empty handed! "I hope I never have the misfortune to be on the opposite side of the bench to you in a court of law." I laughed. I became accustomed to them being there in the mornings, always bright and cheerful, and with some adventure to tell of the night before.

The painting was coming on well; one evening, Sara was painting until the light failed when suddenly she heard a terrible blood-curdling shriek. Her thoughts turned to Dracula movies, and she froze on the spot. As the shriek faded, there was a whoosh of wings and footsteps pattering just above her head in the partly boarded attic. She dropped her brushes and bolted! Next morning when I arrived they were still sitting in the caravan, too scared to enter the barn, for fear of what they might find. We all entered with trepidation, and there sitting on a high beam glaring down at us with wide, evil eyes, was a beautiful barn owl. He took fright and whooshed around the barn before escaping through a porthole high up in the roof. Five minutes later we heard him return. We found a ladder, and climbed up, poking our heads into the boarded part of the attic; there it was, asleep in the corner. There were many regurgitated waste balls on the boarding below; it was obviously an old nest. I managed to reach an old moldy ball; it was dry and did not smell at all. I broke it open, and inside were the bones of some small unfortunate mouse or vole. Why the owl was awake and sitting on the exposed beam in broad daylight, I have no idea. I had never seen it before, although I had heard the screech of owls many times when we lived there in our caravan. I felt very honoured to have an owl in my attic.

Sara and Nikki were also fairy godmothers to little Robin, the kitten. One night, they heard the screech of brakes; their first thought was for the two little kittens, which they loved and spoiled terribly. Sure enough, there was Robin lying in the road. He seemed badly dazed, but not injured. They picked him up and kept him warm. He slept in Nikki's arms, inside her sleeping bag, and the next morning he was fine, but if they had not been there, it could have been the end of his little life.

Sara just managed to finish the painting. We asked an English friend of ours, who was going to a big party in Lisbon, to give them a lift; he said he would take them to the party, and then give them a lift to the airport the following day, which they were thrilled about. But I was going to miss them. Sara admired a tie-dyed T-shirt, I was wearing - she was wearing an old paint splattered one. "Swap." I said, taking it off and giving it to her without hesitation.

The next morning there were no welcoming shouts, or cup of coffee, just the horses whinnying for their breakfast. The painting was good and attracted many people. Horses were very much a novelty in this area, and sometimes families would visit just to see them. We were happy to do this and one day a man brought two little immaculately dressed twins to see the horses. The little girls were more interested in playing with the kittens. They particularly liked Robin, who was a very affectionate kitten; they cuddled and played with him whilst I was talking to their father. Craig, who by now spoke the language well, was very concerned about what the little girls were saying. When they left, he said. "Mum, those little girls asked their dad if they could take Robin home." Apparently, after their pleading with him, the father had said, "Maybe later."

I thought very little about it, but Craig would not forget the incident. The next morning, Robin had disappeared. The kittens were three months old; they used to go out on their own, but were always there in the morning for breakfast. By the end of the day, I feared for his safety, and walked along the road on both sides, expecting to find his remains. There was no sign of him anywhere. "I told you those horrible little girls were plotting to take him," remarked Craig sadly. I too felt sad, he was a funny little cat with a doll like round face, and if he didn't like something, he would lay his ears back like a horse!

To make matters worse, about two weeks later, I was giving a private lesson in the sand school, when I heard Craig shout out in horror. I looked up, but could see nothing amiss, then he appeared, sobbing, with Batman held limp in his arms, quite dead. I abandoned the lesson and went to comfort him. It was the first death he had seen; there was hardly any blood, just a trickle from his mouth, he looked as if he were asleep. It was a nasty experience for Craig; the car driver hadn't even stopped.

A couple of weeks later, one month after he had gone missing, little Robin walked in the door! I couldn't believe my eyes. He looked well; someone had been feeding him. I decided to take him home, he would be lonely all on his own, and our house is nowhere near a main road, so he would be much safer.

Craig saw me getting out of the car with a little furry bundle, and came running down the steps. Tears sprung to his eyes when he saw it was Robin. "From now on," I said, "he is going to live here with us and BB." After some thought, we came to the conclusion that it was possible that the little girls' parents had a holiday home in this area, as many people did, and it was possible that they took the kitten as a pet whilst they were here, then on returning to the city, had dropped him off again. They may not have guessed that Robin was Craig's pet, thinking him a stray barn cat. It was a feasible reason for his disappearance, but of course, we will never know for sure.

We had managed to find a farrier. There was a big agricultural college in Coimbra and we knew they bred horses so surely they must have a farrier. We visited the college one day and were introduced to Henrique a short, well built man in his seventies, I couldn't believe it. In England most farriers are young and strong, and charge a fortune; here they seemed to be all old men who charged hardly anything! He said he would cycle to Coimbra station from his house, carrying all his tools and horse shoes, then catch a train to Serpins, our local station, and we would pick him up from there. We agreed a time and day, and the first time, it all went smoothly, although I thought he was going to have a heart attack by the time he finished the third horse.

The next time we needed him, we tried to arrange it by phone. We soon realized that it's a lot harder talking in a foreign language on the phone than in person, we thought he said we were to pick him up at the station at 10.30. Or had he said he would catch the train at 10.30, we knew he was doing something at 10.30! Steve drove to the station to collect him, but no Henrique emerged from the train. Steve waited for the next one, which was 1 hour 20 minutes later...but still no sign of him.

This happened quite a few times over the next few months, it was so frustrating. One time there was a train strike; another time he was ill. It wasn't his fault; he couldn't phone us because we still didn't have a phone. We had asked many times to have a phone connected to our house, but it was a big job, because the telephone company had to supply poles from the nearest village, at their expense. It was always amanhã amanhã.

Our Belgian friend Peggy, from the Góis campsite, offered to be our secretary. Her Portuguese was much better than ours, so she made the arrangements with the farrier for us, and if there was a problem, Henrique phoned her and she would come and tell us. Things ran much smoother after this, and we were most grateful to her. On one visit, Henrique was to shoe Cigano for the first time. "Eu conheço este cavalo" he said (I know this horse.) We told him the story of our buying him at the market. He was highly amused, saying that he had heard about the spectacle but hadn't connected it with us. He said Cigano used to race years ago, but in recent years he had been tethered day and night on a gypsy encampment just outside the city. Poor Cigano, now I knew why he loved his stable so much. The flies and baking hot summers must have driven him crazy. He was a thin-skinned horse, not tough like a cob; he must have frozen in the winter wind and rain. He still wasn't responding to me, although he was very well behaved. He would never touch his food until I had left the stable, and even then he often would not eat it all. He didn't mix well with the other horses either, he was always on his own, and he was happiest left alone in his stable.

Meanwhile Steve had been working well on the house, the upstairs main living room was transformed. He had mended the floor, re-rendered the walls and whitewashed the whole room with Cal (Lime). We made enquiries about the cost of having electricity installed, but the estimate we were given was ridiculously high. Again we needed to have 300 metres of posts installed in the road from the village, but this time it was us who were expected to meet the cost. We couldn't afford it, and decided to look into other power sources. In this land of sunshine, surely solar power would be a viable alternative, but for the moment we would have to be content with our gas lamp and the romance of candles.

Our nearest neighbour, Francisco, was a short, barrel chested little man who looked as strong as an ox; he was about 55 years old with a ruddy complexion and a lovely smile that crinkled his soft sparkly brown eyes. He had a moustache, long curly greying side burns, and was never without his flat cap. Steve called at his house one day which was distanced by a finger of pine forest from our house, and on seeing him without his cap, didn't recognize him, he was completely bald and where the flat cap sat, his scalp was as white a snow! Francisco was a constant source of surprise to us in the first year that we came to live here. He told us that he had lived in our house when he first married and had his first two children under our roof; one day during the early 1970's, there was an earthquake which shook the house so badly that the roof and end wall started to cave in. His wife was alone in the house with her two babies; she just picked them up and ran for her life. She must have been so scared, no wonder they never moved back in! They only moved to the next village because he still farmed the land around our house, and didn't want to give it up. Many years after the earthquake, when his sons were grown up, they went to work in the building industry in Switzerland where the wages were much higher. They financed a nice little concrete house with all mod-cons for their parents; although Francisco still insisted on having an outdoor kitchen. He was usually to be found veiled in smoke, and with a glass of wine in his hand, making his delicious black puddings and smoked sausages.

No one had lived in our house or done any repairs on it since the earthquake, until Adam had bought it about 20 years later. Unfortunately Adam and Francisco didn't get on, there was a running feud between them which started when Adam had committed the deadliest of sins, without realizing it he had built his hole in the ground type toilet on part of Francisco's land. The land is often divided up into small parcels with no obvious boundaries – to us anyway. The locals know every rock and twig on their land and woe betides the stranger who picked up a nice looking rock to take home for a rockery! It could be the corner stone of someone's plot. Occasionally you might have found a dab of paint on a stone, but most of the time there was nothing to suggest a boundary: it was all handed down through generations of local knowledge.

Francisco did not scold or argue with Adam over his misdemeanor, which was purely caused by bad communication because Adam didn't speak the language well when he first arrived. He wasn't even aware of the crime he had committed, but the next day one of Adam's newly planted trees disappeared and miraculously re - appeared in Francisco's garden. He did not try to hide the tree; it was there for all to see in the middle of the front garden! The feud continued when Francisco built a crow scarer 50 metres from Adam's bedroom window (now our bedroom window). The contraption was hand made from an old Marvel dried milk tin turned upside down with a shaft across the top. A vane mounted on the rear end kept the blades, which were made from shaped pieces of tin, (a bit like a child's windmill) permanently facing into the wind. Two small weights, probably nuts (as in nuts and bolts) were attached on short strings to the spinning shaft, and as it span, they drummed on the upturned milk tin. The whole ingenious apparatus was set on a twenty-foot pole. It was supposed to scare the crows from his newly planted seeds; he also made a scarecrow dressed in a pair of old overalls and wearing a motorbike crash helmet. From the crutch of the overalls, hung the most enormous erect penis! I never ventured close enough to decipher exactly what it was made from, but it was still there when we moved in. Various articles of clothing were draped around the tiny field, and plastic drink bottles were strategically placed on twenty-foot canes that wavered in the slightest breeze; he certainly seemed to have an obsession against crows.

The clanging windmill made one hell of a din when the wind was blowing through the valley. Luckily the winds were thermal and usually died down at night. However one night the wind howled all night long and poor Adam could not sleep through the incessant clattering of the windmill, which went on hour after hour. Finally he got up, in an absolute rage and stark naked, he ran outside, picked up a big rock, and hurled it at the contraption. Silence! He had hit it, and the thing fell to the ground. War was declared. Francisco built it back up and although Adam tried, he never managed to knock it down again.

When we moved in we were determined to get on with our new neighbour. We were lucky that there was not much wind that May/June when the windmill was in action, so it did not annoy us too much. We bought produce from his wife Maria, and generally tried to get along with him. Maria, loved to mother Craig, all of her four children were grown up; she seemed to have an unending supply of chocolate hidden in her apron pockets, so he was always happy to see her. But as far as Francisco was concerned we were still on trial.

He had another trick up his sleeve. He was always telling us stories about the wild pigs called Javalis. They came down from the hills at night and ate all his young maize plants. "Life is so hard on a poor farmer," he told us woefully, as he leaned heavily on the field gate. "The javalis and the crows take everything he plants." he complained, pushing his flat cap to the back of his head and wiping sweat from his face with his grubby handkerchief.

He still owned the field next to ours down by the river, and his new corn crop was just shooting with young succulent stems. One night, about midnight, we were just drifting off to sleep when there was an almighty bang. We both jumped out of bed thinking someone had been shot. Fortunately Craig just slept on. It would take more than a gun shot to wake him.

There was not a sound, it was a very dark night, Steve dragged on some underpants and slippers and grappled for the torch in the darkness, then timidly opened the bedroom door, which led directly onto the front porch. He crept down the steps into the yard while I searched for something heavy to use as a truncheon, suddenly, I heard voices. I froze. "Boa noite," (good night) said a familiar voice. I looked out of the window and could make out two unmistakable forms, one was Steve; tall and thin in his underpants, and the other was the squat form of Francisco, his face beaming into the torch light in amusement. "No problem, only the javalis," he assured Steve.

About 2 am, we were awakened by another bang, then another. We were very upset and the next morning we walked along to his house to ask him in our best Portuguese, why he was shooting the javalis, which we had been told was illegal, as they were protected. He laughed at us, "Oh I don't kill them, I just frighten them." He then beckoned us outside to show us how he did it: it was yet another of his inventions! He wrapped small amounts of explosive into paper twists, (a bit like the old blue salt twist we used to get in Smith's plain crisps, for any of you old enough to remember!); He put the paper twist of explosive on a large flat stone and picked up an iron bar, about one inch diameter and four feet long, and dropped it onto the explosive; the bang made me jump out of my skin, it was louder than a shot gun.

He kept up this vigil for about tow weeks. We would see him making his way determinedly down to his field just on dark. When did he sleep? He would sit down there all night protecting his crops. Sometimes the explosive didn't go off and we would hear the warning 'clink' as he missed his target and the pole hit the stone, but next try, he would hit the target. BANG. We actually became accustomed to the disturbance; I would vaguely hear it through my sleep, but not waken.

After a few weeks, the plants were high enough, and had grown a coarse stem which was not as appetizing for the javalis or the crows, so the nightly vigil ceased and the crow scarer with its 20 foot pole, which now had an alarming sag, was taken down, overhauled, and stored away ready for next year. Peace reigned – but for how long!

In all other ways Francisco was the perfect neighbour. Throughout the summer and autumn, he brought along buckets of figs, tomatoes, peaches, and was always full of helpful hints on how to salt our olives, and make our own wine from our vines. He told us we were very lucky to have three large cork oak trees on our land, saying the harvested cork was worth a lot of money. The trees were harvested every nine years, and Francisco told us that this was the ninth year, so during the summer, two experts at removing cork from the trees would be touring the area, he promised he would make sure that they called on us to remove the cork bark from our trees. He even taught me how to prepare lettuce! One morning he called to us as we were walking past his house, and beckoned us to follow him into his garden. He cut a huge lettuce and handed it to us; instructing us at the same time to wash the leaves well, pat dry, then add some salt. He pressed his thumb and index finger together to his lips and with a flourish; made a kissing sound! We were growing very fond of him and his wife, and decided that it was not our place to interfere with his self-sufficiency. We must learn to take the good with the bad; if he needed to protect his crops then we would accept it as part of living in the countryside.

I think they began to like us also. When there is a language barrier, it is easy to jump to the wrong conclusions. We thought he was doing things to spite us, but of course this was just our paranoia, he was living his life the way he had always known. The lifestyle of some of the older mountain people had not been affected by modern living yet, their life had probably changed very little over the generations.

One morning we awoke to the sound of scraping on the little country lane that runs past our house. It was Francisco, scraping the gravel from the roadside into little piles about every twenty metres. Later he was back, shovelling them into his trusty wheelbarrow with its ear piercing squeak! What was he up to now? We had a pile of old broken Mediterranean style roof tiles lying in our yard. They had probably been there for years and I'm sure he knew of their existence, but now he had a use for them. He was the grand master of re-cycling, and this morning as he leaned on our wall talking about his favourite subject, the weather, his eyes lit up at the sight of the pile of tiles, would we like him to clear away those scruffy old tiles for us? We were perfectly happy for him to take them, and asked him why he had been cleaning the road earlier. He chuckled, he wasn't cleaning the road, he needed the gravel to make cement, he was building a new bread oven, that's why he needed the tiles; for the interior roof.

We had heard about these ovens and actually had an old ruined one in our woodshed, so we were interested to go and have a look at the logistics because Steve was keen to restore our own. Steve asked Francisco if we could come and see his new oven when he had finished it. "Sim, eu vou lhe avisar" (yes I will let you know) he waved, loading some broken tiles onto his already full wheelbarrow which squeaked in protest all the way home!

A few weeks later we were invited along to Francisco's house. His new bread oven was of a solid construction, built outside in his back yard, it stood about chest high. It was made of stone with thick walls, like a little house. The interior was a small cave with a domed roof like an igloo and a flat floor made of clay, the walls and roof were formed by using many tightly packed small broken pieces of roof tiles. The interior was about one and a half metres diameter, but it had no chimney.

He was preparing the oven for bread making when we arrived, throwing in small sticks and paper waste, he had been feeding it constantly for an hour or so until the whole oven had heated up. Now he raked aside the remaining sticks ready for the breads to be baked directly onto the oven floor.

His wife Maria came out with a large wooden tray, with sloping sides about 3-4 inches deep. We had seen these trays at the markets and wondered what they were for, now we were about to find out. The tray was full of very wet dough. Maria also had two other smaller bowls, one filled with flour and the other empty. She floured her hands, and put a handful of flour in the empty loaf sized bowl, she scooped up some stodgy dough and placed it on top of the flour. She shook the bowl until the stodgy dough formed into the shape of a loaf. Francisco was waiting with a wooden paddle which he placed over the bowl and tipped it upside down so that the bread was now on the paddle. He slid it onto the oven floor. In the time it took him to do that, Maria had another loaf floured and shaped, ready for him to transfer to the oven. Within 60 seconds they had 10 loaves in the oven. Maria had some sliced onions ready and as she scraped up the remaining dough from around the tray, she threw in the onions and mixed it all together before adding this last one to the oven.

Later, when we were back at home, we heard a shout from the top of our drive, (she would never come down and knock on the door) I ran up to see what she wanted. With a big smile she held out a still warm onion broa which is a very heavy bread made with maize and wheat flour. It was delicious.

Another speciality is Chamfana which is meat from an old goat, cooked with red wine and herbs and placed in the still hot bread oven to cook long and slow for hours. Steve found a more modern use for our own newly renovated bread oven; it cooked the most wonderful pizzas!

One of the other villagers, called Carlos, had a field close to us; he was a little surlier, and kept his distance. He was always polite, but not such an extrovert as Francisco, he was probably daunted at the prospect of talking to estrangeiros (foreigners) although our language was improving. Before we went to bed, usually about midnight, we used to walk Toby and the two pups.

We were walking on a path through the woods one night, by torchlight, when a head popped out from behind a tree; it took us by surprise to say the least! It was Fatima, Carlos' wife; she had been dozing at the base of the tree and our torchlight had woken her. "Boa noite," she said sleepily. She was on Javali watch, and had fallen asleep. She was using two saucepan lids, which she banged together to frighten off the boar, which was a lot more sociable than Francisco's explosives! We left her to her uncomfortable slumber and were wondering what we would find next, when from behind a hedge came "BOO." It was Carlos laughing at our startled faces. He was watering his land. Didn't anybody sleep around here?

The river borders all the plots of land that run along the valley on one side. The local council built a concrete channel from the river along the other side of the land so that each farmer had access to water from both sides. The water is siphoned from the river, down the channel, each plot has a wooden trap door built into the channel. When the trap door is lifted, water floods the plot. Even in the middle of summer we have access to as much water for our land as we need; it's so simple, yet works extremely well. To this day the fields are still watered in the same way. The only problem is finding time for your watering when nobody else upriver is using it for himself. I can only assume that was why Carlos was gardening at midnight!

About a month later, Francisco arrived at our house accompanied by two men. These were the specialist cork cutters. After introductions, all three men stared up at the trees, decisively stroking their chins and evaluating their worth. We were left wondering what this valuable crop would be worth when eventually Francisco came over to us and gave us a figure in escudos, (which was the currency up until 1999) of a figure equivalent to about 20 euros. We obviously were not going to become rich on our cork harvest! We were however very interested to watch how the cork was removed from the trees. The men worked quickly using a specialized cork axe to slit the outer bark and peel it away from the tree trunk and main branches. The process is always done by hand, and if the cut is too deep, the tree can be killed. The men told us that trees can live for 500 years, and that they thought our trees were well over 100 years old. Once the cork is removed the tree seems to bleed; it becomes a rusty red colour which fades over time as the new bark starts to grow. The men finished by painting the year onto the tree so that they would know when to return. They are beautiful trees and give us lots of shade, but financially I would not be holding my breath.

CHAPTER 10

PONTE DE LIMA

In 1995, people from this area were not used to seeing foreigners. Even now, not many tourists have discovered the mountain areas of Portugal, preferring to cling to the coast. Mention Coimbra, which is our nearest city, to most foreigners who have visited Portugal and they haven't a clue where it is, yet it is the third largest city, and boasts one of the oldest universities in Europe.

The older people in the villages looked on us as odd, with our blonde hair and strange ways. They couldn't believe that our dogs and cats were allowed in the house, what was the point of having them? Dogs should be chained next to the chicken shed to guard the precious food chain, we were told time and time again. How could we expect our cats to catch mice, when we fed them from a can? And when Paul was staying with us - a man with long hair? Why didn't he cut it?

The best way to cope with being odd was just to wave and smile at everyone. The response was amazing; old ladies dressed in black with baskets of cabbages balanced on their heads, waved carefully, afraid to upset their load, as they went on their way. Groups of youths standing outside bars and cafés, acknowledged us cheerfully. It was as if they had been unsure of us and were waiting for a sign from us that we wanted to be friends.

Sign language has no nationality, and one man that we befriended not long after arriving was proficient in the art. Our Portuguese language at that time was improving but conversation was still difficult, we conversed with Eduardo in sign language, it was great fun.

To tug and wiggle your ear lobe two or three times means something is very good, a restaurant perhaps, or a certain type of grape to grow for the table. Two taps on the side of the nose is a definite no-no. When talking about your husband or wife, you simply tap your third finger on the left hand. Holding your index fingers together, means you, or whomever you are talking about, are a couple. Anything to do with prison, police, or anything illegal, is made clear by making a pattern of prison bars using your two middle fingers on both hands, crossed. Money is discussed by rubbing together the thumb and index finger, and lots of money, by slapping the back pocket of your trousers. He managed to tell us, using hardly any words, that he had once farmed worms (told by wriggling his index finger worm like) on our land. It had been very good and earned him lots of money, but his wife had not been keen on him spending every weekend playing around with worms!

He had a lovely little daughter called Susanna. She was about three years old, and used to stand in front of him on the running board of his motor scooter. She wore no helmet, although he did, which seemed a bit ironic. Susanna loved to watch the horses from the safety of our forecourt, but we could not tempt her to come down the steps to meet them, but she did learn a few words of English. "Black dog Toby" she would say patting him, and "white horse Smartie."

Eventually she allowed her father to carry her down the steps to stroke white horse Smartie. Gradually she gained confidence and would sit on his back. Then after Smartie had walked a few steps, she realized she liked it, and was hooked, we couldn't get her off – she screamed whenever her father tried to remove her. I started giving her short lessons. I had to punch holes nearly up to the top of the stirrup leathers; she looked like a pimple balanced on him. Her father said she had an affinity with Smartie, and dreamed about him at night.

Another Smartie fan was a young girl called Inês who lived in Lisbon. She was 12 years old; her family had a holiday home near to us. She had a deep love of horses but was very nervous. She had to try really hard to conquer her fears. We took it slowly; firstly she would groom him and feed him carrots, getting to know him and losing her fear of being near such a large animal. It was a big step for her when she first mounted Smartie, and walked around on him. She was visibly shaking but had a determination seldom seen in one so young. I knew that as long as everything went smoothly and slowly she would progress at her own pace.

Inês visited again in the summer for two weeks and came for a lesson every day. At the end of her visit she had made such good progress that I agreed to take her out for a ride around the village. I rode Guv and she followed behind on Smartie. Her parents were nearly as excited as she was, and her father drove slowly in front of us, while his wife, from the window of the car, took a video of the whole ride! Inês still comes riding with me whenever she can, we have become good friends, and she is hoping to make a career in equitation.

There were two handsome young Portuguese men who rode with me regularly. Alberto was the local butcher, who being young, fit, and enthusiastic learned to ride very quickly. He would bring a bagful of nice scraps of meat and choice bones for our dogs. The dogs always gave him a rapturous welcome, I wonder why? The other, Henrique was a lawyer; he helped us with the paper work on our house. He was a true anglophile, speaking perfect Queen's English, and putting us to shame.

After riding, one Sunday afternoon, he produced a picnic basket with a china teapot, teacups and saucers, silver spoons, and a silver napkin rack, apologizing for the napkins only being paper. He spread an old family linen tablecloth out on the grass, and served cream cakes and Earl grey tea in the warm sunshine. The hard life of a riding instructor in Portugal!

We had been told of a big horse fair taking place in the north of Portugal. It would be held in September in a town called Ponte de Lima. It would be a long drive in our slow old horsebox, which was not at its best around winding mountain roads, but we decided to go. It was the time of the round up of wild ponies called Garranos from Geres National Park. The young stock were sold off and were the main contributors of the fair but there were also Lusitano horses, donkeys, cows and sheep. It should be a good place to buy a pony. The drive was about 260 kilometres and Steve calculated that it would take six hours to get there on winding mountain roads.

We would have to drive overnight as the fair started early. Two English friends Will and Claire wanted to come with us. Only three people can ride in the cab, so we threw a mattress in the back of our truck and Will and Claire took first turn riding in the back. We left at about 7pm. And drove until 10pm, when we stopped for supper at a roadside restaurant. Afterwards, Craig and I took our turn in the back. We had brought bedding and were soon settled down, the rolling motion and constant drone of the engine sending us easily to sleep.

Steve told me later of their experiences, they had missed the turn off for Porto, which would have bypassed the city, and found themselves crossing the ancient iron bridge through the middle of the city. It was a two-tiered bridge across the river Douro. The city was beautifully illuminated and they could see the famous old Port houses on the south bank, and quaint fisherman's cottages on the steep banks. He said it was quite awesome driving a big truck through mazes of cobbled streets, but we had slept blissfully on. Later they found themselves lost again in Braga, another large town, but eventually arrived in Ponte de Lima at about 2am.

Rowdy people thronging the horsebox awakened me and my immediate fear was that we were surrounded by some sort of gang. I peered sleepily from the groom's door window, and there before my eyes was a fairground in full swing, with us in the middle of it! The whole area was ablaze with lights; people were parading the streets dressed in carnival costumes with big paper mache painted heads, some people were in colourful national dress. A marching band played loud cultural music as Dodgems and Waltzers whirled and swirled their squealing occupants. We were driving at walking pace through the middle of the revellers. There were queues of people at the pop up bars selling Brazilian Caipirinha, and stalls already set up selling horse saddles and all kinds of leather ware; from bridles to beautiful hand crafted shoes, handbags, cowboy hats and much more.

Steve was obviously looking for somewhere to park for the night. Finally we crossed a bridge, which took us to the other side of the river and the engine shuddered to a stop. Craig slept peacefully on in our makeshift bedroom, so I left him there, and jumping down I walked around to the front of the truck.

We had parked on the banks of the river, right next to the market square. The sheep and cattle pens had already been erected; two horses were tied to a tree, obviously their quarters for the night. I was wide-awake and ready to party, but Steve was exhausted; having driven the heavy old truck for seven hours. However the party spirit was infectious, and after a couple of strong coffees at a nearby bar, he had a last burst of energy and wanted to explore. Will and Claire had brought a tent and were pitching it. "We can listen out for Craig, you guys explore" they suggested, so we went for a walk. The night was heavy with cloud; the streetlights threw a dappled beam through the thick mist, which spread upwards from the river. It was a truly beautiful old town with many ancient buildings and more than its share of churches. We strolled over a wide low stone bridge, from which the town got its name. Ponte (bridge) over the river Lima. We got chatting to a young Portuguese couple who had stopped on the bridge for a cuddle. They told us that this was one of the biggest festivals of the year in Portugal, it was called Feiras Novas and had been celebrated since 1826 in honour of 'Our Lady of Sorrows'. "Who was she" I asked. They shrugged, "I think she was the Virgin Mary" hesitated the girl, unsure of her facts. "This bridge is 2000 years old and was built by the Romans" she continued proudly. It seemed that we had missed an amazing firework display; what a pity as I love fireworks! We left them to their embrace and walked slowly back to our truck.

The night's activities were cut short by a heavy shower. Most of the fairground revellers drifted off home in bedraggled costumes, and only a few bars were left open. Typically, one of them was close to our horsebox come bedroom. A group of men were singing and dancing in the rain, too well stoked up on whiskey to worry about the shower. There was music playing inside the bar, and people were shouting and laughing. Steve was so tired that he drifted off to sleep even through the noise. It must have been about 5 am. when everything quietened down and I started to doze.

Almost immediately, I was awakened by the frightened noises of farmyard animals amplified 100 times over, or so it seemed, as the sounds of cows and sheep drifted into my consciousness. They were being unloaded and driven into their pens, with shouts and whistles from their owners. I turned and cuddled up to Steve, "I can't hear any whinnies," I mumbled.

About an hour later, we stiffly got up and dressed. It was quite cold and drizzling heavily. Steve stumbled out of the horsebox, and returned a while later with two cups of steaming coffee, and an orange juice for Craig, who was now jumping around like a springbok; he was very excited at the prospect of us buying a pony. "There's a lot of strange looking horses out there with horns" joked Steve, trying to hide his disappointment at the lack of horses and ponies to be seen.

Will and Claire were still dozing, curled up in their sleeping bags; we arranged to meet them in half an hour for breakfast. Armed with umbrellas, we stepped out into the early morning drizzle. We walked through all the sheep and cows, knowing there were two horses here somewhere, because we had seen them last night.

Then through the misty rain, we heard the neighing of horses. They were at the far end of the market – about fifty of them in all shapes and sizes, mostly wild young ponies from the moors and mountains.

It was not an auction; the animals were either privately owned or being sold by dealers. Feeling happier now, we returned to the café near our horsebox, where our friends were already sipping hot coffee. More people and animals were arriving, by the time we had finished breakfast, it was difficult to jostle our way through the crowd. There were a lot more ponies now, and people were trying them out amongst the crowd. One sight made us all burst into laughter, a huge fat man with a jacket done up much too tightly for his portly belly, was trying out an equally huge fat horse. The horse had the strangest conformation I have ever seen, its legs flapped out sideways as it trotted, making its backside wobble alarmingly from side to side, like a boat on a choppy sea! The old saying that people look like their animals was certainly true here; these two made a perfect match.

Craig spotted a little chestnut pony with a blonde flaxen mane and tail, she looked so pretty and quiet among the throng of shouting dealers and rearing frightened ponies. We approached her owner, who was standing with her. He was a quietly spoken man who told us that he had ridden the little mare twelve kilometres to market before his children awoke. He didn't want to see their faces when they discovered her missing, but he couldn't afford to keep her any longer.

I will never know if this was his sales talk or not, but he had a genuine air about him. The pony was footsore as she had no shoes, but otherwise in good condition, and it was obvious from her calm manner that she had not been ill treated, as so many ponies had been, making them nervous or aggressive.

The owner was happy for us to try her, so Craig jumped on enthusiastically; I led her to an area where there were not so many people, and within minutes he was riding her unaided. "I love her mum, she's brilliant, please let's buy her." We talked to the owner, but he was asking 800 euros for her, which was much too expensive. Reluctantly we walked away.

Most of the other ponies for sale were unbroken youngsters. There were some lovely bigger horses, but we definitely needed a pony for the school. An hour or so later, the little blonde pony was still standing patiently with her owner. I stood back and had a good look at her; she was about 13.1 hands high, strong and stocky. She could easily carry a lightweight adult; after all she had just carried her owner twelve kilometres. I was looking for a real all rounder, one who would stand patiently while children's inexperienced hands practiced putting on saddles and bridles, yet could carry a small adult if needed. Maybe there was a place for her in our ever-growing family.

Claire taught English to Portuguese students, so her command of the Portuguese language was very good. She also loved to haggle! She had done a lot of travelling in Morocco where bartering for rugs or just a small trinket in the markets can take all day, and many cups of sweet, sickly mint tea! This poor little man from the mountains would be putty in her hands.

His eyes lit up as we approached for the second time, he asked Craig if he wanted to ride her again, and helped him to mount. Craig was happy just to sit on her, because she was footsore, as Claire went through her much practised ritual, throwing up her eyes in shock, talking very fast, emphasizing her points with her hands, she was deadly serious. Three times she consistently shook her head and we all turned on our heels, pretending to be interested in some other pony in his eyeshot. He was proving more difficult than we had originally thought, but finally he relented and dropped the price to 500 euros, which was a fair price.

I felt really sorry for him, he was nearly in tears at the thought of parting with his children's pet, or maybe he was just exhausted from his encounter with the pushy English woman!

Craig was over the moon with his new pony, we had to keep emphasizing that she was for the riding school also, not just his personal pet. On our way back to the horsebox, we passed by two beautiful Lusitano stallions being prepared to perform a show. The Portuguese are very proud of their Lusitano horse, and rightly so, they are a great asset to their country. Initially they were bred as war horses but the breed has been refined over the last 30 years, and they are now world-renowned as magnificent dressage horses.

The two stallions called out to our little mare, but she showed no interest, and walked quietly by our side. She walked straight up the ramp of the horsebox without any fuss, and whinnied to Craig when he appeared carrying hay and water for her.

Leaving her to settle, we went back to the hubbub of the fair to eat lunch. We found a large tent, open down one side so that we could shelter from the drizzle, but could watch the comings and goings of the fair whilst we ate. It was usual market food, barbecued chicken and chips or barbecued sardines with cabbage and boiled potatoes. I love sardines, but am not so keen on boiled potatoes and cabbage! We all settled for the chicken. The smells within the tent were wonderful to our hungry noses, but there were leaks in the seams of the tent, we had to keep moving tables until we found a reasonably dry one.

From our restaurant, we could watch people trying out their new acquisitions along the riverbank. Other people just rode up and down to be seen, on beautiful prancing Lusitano horses, adorned in the traditional bullfighting saddles and fancy bridle. Suddenly the river bank was cleared and a group of men riding the native ponies of the region, called Garranos, gathered. The ponies were snorting and leaping on the spot. It was obviously a race. Sure enough, when they were in some sort of line, a gun was fired into the air and they were off. Galloping flat out along the sandy bank, before screeching to a stop, spinning round, and galloping back. Spectacular lunchtime viewing.

We were sitting near the open side of the tent, only feet away from the crowds milling past, so imagine our surprise when, about fifteen people, men, women, and children, riding highly trained Lusitanos paraded, through the crowds. The horses were executing a high stepping very controlled trot, with necks arched and frothing mouths. The men were dressed in black breeches with white frilly shirts, black waistcoats, and black wide brimmed hats. The women were dressed identically, but wore long skirts and rode sidesaddle. The horses looked so big and powerful, especially to us in our seated position. I could reach out and touch their flanks as they passed our table.

After lunch the sun broke through, illuminating the broad green valley. The veil of misty rain lifted and we could see our surroundings more clearly. The river Lima meandered through a wide fertile valley, surrounded by mixed forest which in this autumn light revealed shimmering patches of gold. As the cloud lifted, shafts of sunlight caressed the whole valley. Wistfully, we wished we could stay longer and explore this beautiful area, but time was against us and we had not seen all the horses and ponies for sale yet. We promised ourselves that one-day we would return for a holiday and stay awhile.

We were drawn to a crowd of people who had gathered to admire a newly arrived horse. It was a four-year-old mare, extremely beautiful and immaculately turned out. She really stood out amongst the unkempt wild ponies around her. We could not make out if it was a girl or a boy showing her. He or she had a chaste Latin profile with short black hair tapering into a long neck and very tall slim immaculately clothed body. They made an elegant pair, but the asking price for the horse was 10000 euros, well above our pocket!

Behind us, being dragged along, was the most sorry sight I had seen for many a year. A poor old cow, just skin and bone, with open sores and wounds all over her body. Her back legs were buckling under her from the sheer effort of having to move, every step looked torturous. If I had a gun, I would have shot her there and then to put her out of her misery, but instead we all stood and stared in horror. Other people joined us, including a group of hardened Portuguese dealers. You would have expected them to be unshockable, but they were furious. They grabbed the man, who was prodding the cow into action and an almighty row broke out. We joined in as well as we could in our pidgin Portuguese. The old man and his cow were jeered from the market.

Our eyes were next drawn to a new horsebox arriving with much stamping and excitable whinnying coming from inside. As the ramp went down, a lovely skewbald (brown and white) foal of about nine months was led down. He was as full of life as the poor old cow was near to death. His brown markings on his white body were symmetrical on both sides. He looked out over this new scene with arrogance beyond his years. He was gorgeous, there seemed to be a lot of interest in him, skewbald horses were rare in Portugal, I hoped he would find a loving knowledgeable home.

Next to him was a large truck owned by a dealer. He had about twenty wild foals and yearlings, recently rounded up from the national park of Gerês. He was a bully of a man, holding on to the little ones' tails, showing off as they bucked and tried to get away. I suppose most of them were sold for meat, similar to the moorland sales in England. The wild ponies were all Garranos. They originate from the north of Portugal and grow to about 13 hands high. They are a strong highly-strung breed, often seen pulling heavy weights between the shafts. A Dutch couple were also looking at the ponies, they told us that they had been on a day trek riding Garrano ponies through the mountains, they were amazed at their stamina and agility. Sadly the breed are in decline as their use on farms and as pack animals has been replaced by modern equipment.

We noticed a large void around one pony and we soon found out why. As soon as we tried to approach her, her legs kicked out in all directions like a windmill. She was so quick in her movements that it was impossible to get near her. Eventually I managed, and once I had hold of her rope, I thought I was safe, but no, she fired from both ends! Her teeth were as proficient as her back legs. I spoke gently to her, but her eyes were blind with panic. She was about 15 months old and as pretty as a picture, her colour was very dark brown; almost black, with a white star that trickled on half way down her face before fading out. I knew she would not grow a lot more, and that we had not meant to buy two ponies, but she was so cute and I felt so sorry for her, she had obviously been very traumatized during her young life.

"No Sandra," our friends were saying, "you can't buy a pony that kicks and bites, when you expect it to be handled by children." Of course they were right, but Steve had fallen in love with her too! "Can we dye her mane purple, like a 'my little pony'," he laughed. "She's a real little poppet, but I'm glad it's you not me that has the job of teaching her manners!"

"She's young, I'll teach her how to behave," I said and silently hoped! The price was 300 euros, and we were only able to haggle it down to 280 euros, which luckily included the tatty hand made head collar-lead rope. She was very reluctant to leave the other ponies, and put up quite a fight for such a petite pony. When we reached the horsebox, and she caught sight of our other little mare; she almost galloped up the ramp dragging me behind. Our little mare whinnied to her and they nuzzled each other, becoming firm friends in an instant. We gave her some hay and water, and left them in peace.

It was almost 2 pm. We were all beginning to tire, and we still had the long drive home. We wandered through the maze of stalls selling just about everything, from a tea strainer to booking up the stallion of your choice for your mare's next foal. The stallions were parading up and down showing off their paces, but we had no need for their services as we had our own stallion. He may be old, and a bit wonky, but he had intelligence and a wonderful kindness, and we certainly had no plans to breed foals!

We wanted to buy a saddle, and found four stalls selling horse tack in fierce competition with each other. Just the place to find a bargain. We were looking at a saddle on one stall, and a little old lady came up behind us, digging us in the ribs to get our attention. "Anything that dirty Spanish gypsy offers you, I will offer cheaper," she crowed through black gapped teeth. The quality of the leather was not brilliant, but the prices were incredibly cheap. They even allowed us to take the saddle back to the horsebox and try it on the pony for size. Will was not so lucky, he wanted a pair of cowboy boots in size 12. The biggest size he could find was size 9. The Portuguese are not a tall race; they stared at him as if he was abnormal to have size 12 feet!

Back in the horsebox, we now faced a new quandary. How were we going to drive out of this place? Steve had not got a clue. He weaved the lorry through all the horseboxes and trailers searching for a way out. We caught sight of a policeman who came to our rescue. He directed us forward, but another vehicle was coming in the opposite direction with no room to pass, so the policeman directed us into the crowd, telling us we would have to drive through the still thronging market! There was nothing else for it, so we made our way at walking pace through the crowds. Some stall owners actually had to remove tent guy ropes so that we didn't pull down their whole stall, but nobody seemed to mind, everyone was in high spirits. Old men, standing drinking in the outdoor cafés along route, put down their glasses and helped clear the way ahead for us, waving their walking sticks importantly, and shouting to people to make way for us.

Once we were on the journey home, I decided to start the little wild pony's education straight away. Craig and I rode in the back with the two ponies. They had wooden partitions between them, just a little wider than their bodies and about four feet high, giving them something to lean against around corners.

I chatted to the ponies gently stroking the smaller wild one; she hated it, but could not kick me, only the partition. Her ears were laid flat against her head, but she was tied quite short, so she couldn't bite me. Gradually she relaxed, realizing I was not going to go away, but was not hurting or threatening her in any way.

By the time we arrived home, she was used to my smell and touch; she allowed me to run my hand down her neck, over her back, and as far down her legs as I could reach. She also consented to me stroking her face without trying to bite my hand off! I was pleased with her progress; it had been worth all the discomfort. Craig who had been petting his pony, had chosen her name - Foxy, and I named 'my little pony' - Tessie.

We led the ponies into the sand school for the night, fed them some hay and left them buckets of water. We then had to feed and water, by torchlight, five irate horses, who were not used to having to wait until after dark for their dinner. They were extremely fractious, especially Guv, who liked to stick rigidly to routine.

The fact that they lived in a lovely grassy field was beside the point, he had missed his breakfast, and I was late for supper, he was in no mood to forgive me. We had given him the nickname of 'Alien' because he was normally such a nice tempered gentle horse, but he had an inner being that emerged at mealtimes. When 'Alien' took over, he became ugly and fearful, laying his ears back and tossing his head. He snapped violently at the air around him like a crocodile! We all, including the horses, gave him a wide berth at feed times.

CHAPTER 11

WINE MAKING

During September we had our first experience of picking our own grapes and making wine; we had some vines at home and also some at the quinta where the horses were living. We had resurrected them from under years of bramble growth when we had cleared the land. I have always enjoyed fruit picking; I find it therapeutic. I used to love walking on the South Downs as a child, picking wild blackberries.

We invited a few volunteers to help us with the promise of a few bottles of the finished product, and had a very enjoyable day's labour. I don't know how many kilos we picked but by the end of the day, our shorts and T-shirts looked a very fashionable tie dyed pink, and every time I brushed a hair or insect from my face, I added another line of war paint, but it was worth it!

We borrowed a machine from Francisco that resembled an old fashioned mangle, called an esmagadora. It had a large wooden funnel attached to the top, and you simply fed the grapes into the funnel, the juice and skins flowed into a barrel underneath. We added no preservatives or chemicals, but just left it for two weeks to ferment, before siphoning off the juice into another old oak barrel that we had found in our basement. We were thrilled to find we had made 150 litres of red wine. A wine buff would probably turn his or her nose up at our brew, but we were proud of our achievement. For a first effort, it was drinkable and free. We resolved to plant some white grapes so that in a few years we could make white wine, or mix the two and have rose, that is if we could refrain from eating them all first!

The skins and dregs, we gave to Francisco, who made Aguardente, which is the Portuguese version of the spirit made all over Europe from the skins and dregs of wine making. The French call it Eau de Vie, the Italians Grappa. Basically it is a raw 40% brandy which when left to age can be very tasty, but in its home made form is barely drinkable at it's best, and at its worst it is like brain cell killing firewater, yet we are constantly assured by the locals that to drink it for breakfast with strong coffee aids the digestion! Aguardente is distilled in a large copper vessel called an alambique. A low fire is built underneath, and in time the pure "rocket fuel" drips slowly from the nozzle. I'm not at all sure how legal it is, when our neighbour persuaded us to take a bottle home to try, he told us to hide it under the seat of the car!

A lovely lady called Mafalda had heard of our arrival in Portugal and turned up at our house one day in October in a taxi. Paul, my elder son, was staying with us again, and Mella was over for her half term break from college in London. Paul welcomed Mafalda into the garden. He was collecting dry washing from the line, and had a pair of underpants in his hand. Being an extrovert, he couldn't talk only with his voice, but used his hands as well. Whilst introducing himself to her, and chatting in general, the underpants were flying in all directions! Mafalda was a very well-to-do lady, but luckily she had a sense of humour, she joked for many years about Paul and his underpants! She had worked in London as a young girl, and had met and married her Portuguese husband there. The first of her six children had been born in London, unfortunately her husband was no longer alive, and her children had all left home, leaving her rather lonely.

Mafalda invited us all to her house for dinner; she lived in a very old mansion, crystal chandeliers hung from the ceilings. The entrance from the street was very grand, but decaying. Inside was a large entrance hall, with some beautiful antique furniture, leading to a wide old wooden staircase, with pictures of ancestors on the walls. Mafalda led us into her lounge, the wallpaper was handmade, she thought it was about 100 years old, sadly it was starting to peel in places and I couldn't help but notice that the decorative plaster ceiling had signs of mould; as if water was seeping through. An ornate marble fireplace drew our eyes to a large framed painting above it, depicting her six children. I felt as though her whole life was in this beautiful room. It was crammed with antiques, and her vase collection was quite amazing; I felt rather nervous in the company of my rowdy family, and was relieved when a young girl knocked and entered to announce dinner.

The dining room was more simply furnished. A chandelier hung over the long oak table, which was surrounded by solid oak chairs with studded leather seats. There was so much cutlery on the table that Craig raised his eyebrows and glanced at me with a worried expression on his face! The meal was fantastic starting with a delicious home made soup, and followed by the Portuguese equivalent of our Sunday roast, called Cozido à Portuguesa. Mafalda had boiled four different meats in a saucepan, with onions and garlic. Beef, pork, chicken, chouriço (spicy sausage) and farinheira which looks like a large pale pork sausage, but in fact is made of pork fat, flour and wine. It is quite unappetizing to my palate, but most Portuguese love it. When the meats were all cooked, she removed them from the pan and added potatoes, carrots, and cabbage to the meat stock. We had become accustomed to drinking the local rough wine, but today for a treat, Mafalda opened a vintage bottle from her cellar.

The rich red wine brought a flush to my cheeks. We were all enjoying Portuguese cooking at its best, but she had another surprise in store for us. "What do you think we have for dessert?" she asked with a cheeky grin, "Baba de camelo." We were all really full, but the bowl of dessert now being presented on to the table, raised an appreciative "Mmmmm" from us all. "Maybe just a little bowl, it looks so delicious, what is it?" I asked. "It translates as camel's spit!" she giggled. She had a lot of fun in her for her age and loved to shock us. It had the required effect, "Oh that's disgusting" voiced Paul and Craig together, "please say it's not true, it smells yummy". Mafalda could hold out no longer, and as she served us all she told us the ingredients were condensed milk and lots of eggs, but definitely no camel spit!

We had many memorable meals with Mafalda, she was a great hostess and a fantastic cook. On another occasion we had been invited for an end of summer barbecue in her garden. Steve took over the cooking whilst Mafalda and I went for a stroll around her estate. Her fruit trees were laden with ripe apples and pears. Her gardener was picking and storing them away for winter. She was a very generous lady and as well as filling our stomachs with gastronomic delights, she always had something from her garden for us to take home. In early spring it was oranges, clementines and satsumas, later it was peaches or nectarines and in summer she picked us bunches of roses to brighten our home. She also had diospiros trees and a walnut orchard, but my favourite of all was the plump soft juicy black figs, oh, they were so good. We took cuttings for our own garden and after a few years, we had our own supply. I plucked an apple from the tree and bit into the cream flesh, the sweet juices sprang to the surface. I could easily have eaten another, but I didn't want to spoil my appetite.

As we strolled on, the odd autumnal leaf drifted lazily down from her chestnut woods, Mafalda became tense. "We must go back, it's dangerous to be in the woods when the sun goes down, there are javalis living in there." I was quite keen to see some wild pigs, but she was adamant that we must return. "They are very dangerous," she said, "they may attack us." At that moment I caught the tantalizing aroma of barbecued sardines wafting towards us and could see Steve beckoning us to "come and eat."

While we had been walking, Craig had been visiting the gardener who also looked after a few animals, chickens, ducks, and goats. He also had a young dog, called Piloto, who spent his entire life guarding the animals. He was kept on a chain and although he had a nice kennel, we all felt sorry for him. It was common in those days for dogs to be kept in this way, it has now been made illegal, but the law will take time to filter through, especially to the older generation living in the mountains. Craig spent all his time playing and petting the young dog. It was probably the most excitement the poor creature had ever experienced, and tonight he was in for a real treat as Craig ran backwards and forwards with table scraps from our barbecue. It was a lovely evening; as the night closed in, an autumnal breeze picked up; it was a bit chilly. We decided to drink coffee inside, and strolled through a metal archway, which formed a tunnel to her door. It was densely covered in grapevine with ripe grapes hanging pendulously in bunches. The air hung heavy with the scent of sweet ripe grapes, ready for picking.

I was riding Cigano every day, this high stepping horse had incredible reserves of energy, and was very strong to ride, but I loved him. Even his walk was much faster than the other horses; I had to keep halting him to wait for them to catch up. This made him irritable and want to move on faster, so it was a vicious circle, but he was a challenge and I enjoyed riding him immensely. He still showed no sign of being at ease with me, he never welcomed me or snuffled my pockets and although he had put on weight, and his sores had healed well around his mouth and on his back, he didn't give the impression of being a happy or content horse.

Foxy and Tessie had settled in well, they were great friends, Tessie was still a bit aggressive but so pretty. Foxy had an endearing nature, but she was born to eat! Work was a foreign word to her, in English or Portuguese! She was very lazy and stubborn. One day I led her into the sand school complete with her new saddle and bridle, but luckily no rider, and she crumpled to the ground, just lying in the warm sand! Her last owner and his children must have kept her as a pet, but now she must learn to work. Both of these young ladies loved Silver, they would stand outside his stable door, waiting for him to show some interest in them; like groupies at the stage door, but following true to form, his impeccable manners kept his ardour at bay.

Roxy had proved totally unsuitable in a riding school situation. He refused to stand quietly whilst people mounted. He would stand nicely while they patted and said hello to him, then wait until they put their foot in the stirrup before running backwards, even with me holding him, kicking out at the other horses who were standing patiently, and generally causing havoc.

I was concentrating on, and enjoying riding Cigano, and maybe Roxy's nose was put out of joint. Maybe he felt a touch jealous, I don't know, but his behavior sunk to an all time low. Two Dutch ladies called Anja and Flor had been riding with me for a few months. They were good riders and sometimes liked to ride out without me to guide them. They liked to explore on their own rather than always being led. I trusted them and I trusted Guv and Smartie. Everything was fine until one day Guv was lame; Anja asked if she could ride Roxy. I knew she was a confident rider so dubiously I agreed.

They wanted to go for two or three hours on their own, but after only about one and a half hours, I heard hoof beats on the road. Going out to meet them, I could see poor Anja dismounted and grimly hanging on to Roxy's bridle. He was leaping into the air, tossing his head. "Look mum, I've been bad again" he was saying, showing off and thoroughly enjoying himself. Flor and Smartie arrived a few minutes later. The girls explained that once they had reached the top of the range (where Sarah and I had galloped all those months before) Roxy had obviously remembered, and started pulling very hard on the reins, tossing his head and attempting to rear. Anja had become frightened and dismounted, then she had led him all the way home, down very steep inclines; the poor girl was absolutely shattered. Needless to say she never asked to ride him again!

I had learned a lesson in how not to run a business and vowed to keep Roxy away from my customers in the future. Unfortunately my memory is short and a few months later a young man, called Diogo, who rode with me occasionally, asked if he could bring two friends. He promised me they could ride well, and was so keen that I agreed. "Can I ride Roxy?" Diogo asked. "Yes, and your friends can ride Guv and Smartie". Diogo was not a technically brilliant rider, but he had good natural balance and he was strong!

We set out with me leading on Cigano; Roxy was in a quiet docile mood, and everything was going well. We had a nice canter through a pine forest, the needles making a soft surface for the horses' hooves. "That was great" they shouted, they were in high spirits and we were all enjoying ourselves. Diogo lit a cigarette. "You cannot smoke a cigarette and ride Roxy" I joked. Roxy, realizing that Diogo had relaxed, and was only holding the reins with one hand, saw his chance and performed a perfect pirouette before lunging forward into a flat out gallop. He flashed past me, and Cigano, who could not bear to be overtaken, pursued him!

Luckily we were on a long uphill track, and Roxy, not being that fit, tired first. Cigano overtook, and once he had regained his lead, he settled down again. Guv and Smartie came cantering up behind at a more sedate pace. "He's maluco," (crazy) shouted Diogo, grinning from ear to ear, "I love him."

One morning in early October, I heard the familiar sound of Paulo the postman's motorbike. It spluttered to a stop at the top of our drive. "Bom dia!" I cried, running to meet him. It was always a pleasure when he visited, although I couldn't understand all he had to say because his accent was very thick. He was always cheerful and loved to gossip, and of course living as we were, without electricity, mortgage, telephone, or any other modern day trappings, we didn't have any bills!

Letters were nearly always from friends or family, Paulo handed me the letter; his round ruddy face looked sad so I asked him if he was alright. He shook his head and said that his mother who was 90 years old had been taken into hospital after a fall. I told him I was so sorry to hear that, he gave me a half hearted wave, and sped off. The letter was from my sister Jenny; I opened it eagerly, she was not a regular letter writer, but once she picked up a pen she could not put it down. (she was even worse on the phone) She wrote pages and pages, mostly about her two horses, one of which was Tawny, who we had left behind with terrible colic at Plymouth. Thankfully he had totally recovered but it was a shame he hadn't made it here, he would have been a great asset to us; and he would have kept Roxy in check! The reason for this letter was my father's impending 70th birthday. My family were planning a surprise party for him; my mother would help out with the cost of the airfares for Craig and I, and the whole thing would be kept secret from my dad.

The tickets were booked; it was to be Craig's first aeroplane flight. He was so excited and counted down the days to take off. Steve would have to stay behind and look after the horses, dogs, and cats. I felt mean leaving him behind, but at that time, we had to accept that it was impossible to have holidays together; one of us must always stay behind to care for all the animals.

Craig's excitement was infectious and once at Lisbon airport, I had to admit, I hardly gave Steve or the animals a thought. It was so enjoyable to watch the wonder on the face of my child making his first flight, to see the earth below becoming smaller and smaller, the cars shrinking to the size of his own toy cars and the towns and fields set out like a patchwork quilt. Not being regular air passengers, we had not thought to book a window seat, but the lady who occupied it was very gracious, and offered to change seats. I think she was pleased to take the aisle seat, she seemed very nervous and fingered her rosary beads for the whole journey. Craig had not realized that the wings of the aeroplane were flexible. He was certain the wing was loose and about to fall off! He especially loved going above the clouds, which were gathering in increasing volume as we neared England. It was getting dark at Heathrow, everything looked grey. Some things never change.

We had no idea who was meeting us. We couldn't see her, but we heard her! The screech of my sister, calling, and waving frantically. Hers was not the only familiar face, my mother, brother Richard, his wife Jean, and their children Tom and Emily, had all come to meet us. Craig was unwillingly swallowed into the arms of his grandmother, and smothered in kisses. As soon as he saw an escape route he was off, laughing and joking with his cousins. It was a tearful re-union exactly one year after we had left. I wished my dad could have been there, but of course that would have ruined his birthday surprise.

My parents had been divorced for many years, but stayed good friends, my mother would not miss his birthday party for anything, in fact she and Jenny were the main instigators of the event. As we stepped outside the airport the freezing cold night air struck me. Winter had not arrived in Portugal yet. By the time we reached Brighton it was raining. I was definitely back in England.

The next morning we visited friends and relatives. I had forgotten the fast pace of life, and the volume of traffic. On our little Portuguese country lane, I was more likely to meet an oxen drawn cart than a motorcar! It was lovely to see Tawny again; my sister's horse which we had left behind at Bristol Veterinary college. He was looking fantastic; back to full health. Jenny had loaned him to a mother and daughter who both loved him to bits. He was a lucky boy, it could have all ended very differently.

The day of the party arrived and there were great discussions on how Craig and I should enter to give the most impact. I rather fancied jumping out of a huge cake, throwing my arms into the air, and shouting "SURPRISE", but this met with no response. My father had a twin sister; they didn't see each other very often, especially as they had got older, because they lived a long way apart.

Her son, my cousin, whom I had not seen for years, was to bring her to Brighton. She also knew nothing of the party. We planned for Dad to meet his sister first, in a quiet bar, and then the two of them would be ushered into the function room where the party was, to the chorus of "Happy Birthday." After this Craig and I were to materialize from our hiding place. I was scared stiff, I am useless at that sort of thing and knew I would cry.

Everything went as planned, I will never forget my dad's face when Craig and I entered the room. For a split second I wondered if we had done the right thing, after all he was 70, and it was obviously a big shock. But after momentarily looking a bit unstable, his face broke out into a huge smile, and he hugged us both so tightly. I was crying, so was Craig, and half the people in the hall, even the girls behind the bar! We had a wonderful party, singing and dancing until the early hours. It was lovely to be back in the bosom of my family. Mella and Paul were there with their boy and girl friends. We were all together, except for Steve of course, who was "home alone".

Back in Lisbon, Craig and I were expecting to catch the coach home, but as we came out of the arrivals hall, I saw the tall slim frame of our friend Sam, then from behind a pillar stepped Steve. "Surprise," he laughed, hugging both Craig and I together, "I've been so lonely without you." I suddenly realized how much I had missed him, and Portugal, after only one week away. We had been so busy that the week had flown by, but now, seeing his open arms and smiling face I realised what a big part of me had been missing.

"Sam's mum is arriving on another flight so we thought we would save petrol and journey together," explained Steve. "Great, do we have time for a coffee?, I've never met your mum Sam, what's she like?" I asked. "Oh, you'll see soon enough," he answered guardedly!

Beatrice was easy to spot, a large, upper class lady, immaculately dressed with hair newly permed, and an authoritative manner. She was almost dismissive towards Sam, and complained about the car he drove, the way he dressed, the food on the airline; poor Sam, how was he going to put up with her for a month? Her husband had been a very successful businessman, her daughter had done very well for herself, she obviously looked upon Sam as the black sheep of the family.

Sam, trying to impress his mother, pulled in to the most expensive Chinese restaurant in Coimbra. We had never been there before, the food was out of this world, but unfortunately, so was the bill. On the way home, we were pulled over by roadside police. It was just a random stop, but the young policeman approached the left hand side of Sam's English car, thinking the driver was on that side. His mother wound down her window, and the policeman started talking to her in Portuguese.

Beatrice answered in her most haughty voice. "We are English." The poor policeman wilted beneath her gaze, and he waved us on, bowing and lifting his cap, not daring to ask for our papers. We were all holding our sides laughing; she really was quite a character!

There was another surprise awaiting our return to the house. Steve had arranged for his friend Geoff who was a builder, to come while I was away, and together they had built a huge fireplace. It was an amazing surprise; I was thrilled with it. The fireplace wasn't quite finished so we couldn't light it that night, but it was very mild, and I wanted to check out my veranda and make sure it hadn't blown away in my absence!

Three days after my return, winter arrived. It was still nice and warm by day, but at night the temperature fell dramatically. The fireplace became much more inviting than the open veranda. The first night we lit the fire, I couldn't believe the difference it made to the room, shadows danced across the walls, the room was filled with the welcoming smell of pine and eucalyptus wood smoke. Craig had been out collecting chestnuts, and was now knelt before the fire, cooking them in the embers. Our cold draughty barn was becoming a home.

Steve had designed a chimney with two flues; one running downstairs into what would eventually become our kitchen, where we planned to cook on a wood-burning stove.

Towards the end of November the rain started, slowly turning the landscape from the burnt out yellow of summer to bright beautiful green. The forests gave so many shades of green, the eucalyptus trees with their blue green leaves, and the pines with their darker green foliage which contrasted to the lovely soft green of the olive orchards. The medronheiro trees were in full blossom and fruit at the same time, they looked quite stunning with their snow white blossoms with little yellow centres and pendulous red fruits hanging on long stems from the branches. What a shame they didn't taste very nice, but I'm sure the birds and insects were very grateful for this November bounty.

The temperatures were mild, with long sunny spells between the rains. The grass was growing as I looked at it. The horses enjoyed the sudden disappearance of the flies that had been attacking them with kamikaze style ruthlessness during October. Now life was good for them, new grass to eat and gentle rain on their backs. They all put on weight and looked well.

Foxy unexpectedly came into season, she started flirting outrageously with Silver, turning her bottom to him and lifting her tail to expose herself. At first he tried to escape, and avoided her when they were in the field together, but she was a woman on a mission, she followed him relentlessly wherever he went. If he tried to hide behind a bush she would be there to meet him on the other side. Poor old boy, I felt a bit sorry for him, perhaps he was past it (the vet had recently aged him at about 30 years old) or perhaps he had never had his chance when he was younger and now didn't know what to do. After a few days of flirting, she tired of him and things quietened down again.

When mares are in the presence of a stallion, they repeatedly come into season until they are pregnant. Normally this happens in early spring through to late summer. With an eleven-month gestation, this means that the foal has a good chance of being born in the following springtime, when the grass is good and the worst of the weather is over. A few weeks later Foxy came into season again. She tried the same chat up lines and this time Silver showed a bit more interest. He would sniff all down her neck giving her gentle little nibbles, like kisses. Then he would raise his head upwards and curl his top lip as if praying for help!

One day whilst Craig and I were watching this courtship, he became more demanding, sniffing under her belly and biting all down her back legs; she loved it. "Does Dad bite your legs like that?" Craig joked. Suddenly Silver's penis hardened and without further ado, he tried to mount her. Alas his arthritic knees let him down, Foxy; though desperate to please him, couldn't help taking a step forward as he clumsily mounted her. This was enough to unbalance him and he almost fell off, exhausted.

I left them together, and this pattern continued every ten minutes or so. I was impressed by his stamina, but worried about the strain on Foxy's back, so sadly I separated them. "We'll try again in the spring," I promised the jilted Foxy!

CHAPTER 12

ONE YEAR IN PORTUGAL

The rain continued but it became colder. The mountains surrounding us took on an eerie and mysterious aura, often cloaked in bloated black clouds that would burst, spilling heavy outbreaks of rain. The result was waterfalls springing from previously dry rocks, and the most vibrant rainbows I have ever seen. In the cold morning air, the river was veiled in mist; which would rise and fall, thicken and thin, like a ghost floating effortlessly above gushing water as it meandered through the valley.

It was now time to pick our olives. We had two large trees, and a few smaller ones. The largest tree I measured with a tape at about 200 years old. The olives were falling from the branches made heavy by the rain and becoming spoiled or eaten by insects on the ground. We put on raincoats and braved the elements, picking up all the good ones from the ground. Then we placed a large piece of sacking around the trees and using long sticks, we hit the branches to shake off all the loose olives onto the sacking. This left only a few stubborn olives on the trees, which had to be picked by hand. We took them to the local olive mill to be weighed and pressed. The result was 150 kilos of olives and 15 litres of cold press olive oil. It was like green gold! We gave a few bottles away to visiting family and friends, but the rest we greedily hid away for ourselves. Olive crops are more or less bi-annual so the precious nectar had to last us for two years.

As Christmas approached an air of despair settled over us, me in particular. It would be my first Christmas without Paul and Mella. I sent off cards, and made up parcels for the family in England, but my heart wasn't in it. Money was also a growing problem. We had earned hardly anything since the end of summer, yet the horses were eating more hay than ever as the weather deteriorated from bad to worse. I had never seen such rain. Hailstones fell covering the ground in icy balls that crunched underfoot. The rain was relentless leaving the fields at Quinta da Ribeira where the horses were still living, six inches under water and we actually had water weed growing where there had been grass. The only plant that thrived was the dock, which sprang up everywhere. Apparently the seeds of the dock plant can lie dormant for 80 years just waiting for a chance like this to spring into life, we were told it was the worst rain for 80 years so maybe there was truth in that.

The horses would slosh around in this quagmire for a couple of hours to stretch their legs. They seemed quite fascinated with their new water park and would paw the ground splashing water out from under them. With no grass to eat the novelty soon wore off and they would retreat to the comfort of their stables. Our lovely new sandschool was not only flooded but had water bubbling up from underground streams that we'd had no idea were even there.

The river below our house, changed its character as rain gushed down from the mountains. It became murderous; overpowering anything that stood in its path. The river running through Góis, burst its banks and the pretty riverside wooden café, where we had sat idly sipping cold beers in summer, fell victim to the rising torrent and was sent crashing down the river, followed by an ice cream stand, coke machine, wooden tables and white plastic chairs that had all been stored inside.

Our house is only about 3kilometres from Góis as the crow flies; and from our veranda, we watched all the debris from the café come hurtling past our house – quite spectacular. Our weir, on which I lay sunbathing in summer, was now a deluge of white water. Everything that had given itself up to the force of the river was sent crashing over the weir. Uprooted trees were swirled around in a whirlpool at the bottom of the weir, before being spat out through the spray and floating on towards the sea. We were grateful to have a dry roof, and a roaring fire as our thoughts turned to cake...in particular Christmas cake!

Steve loved to cook, he was never happier than when he was trying to improve on old and trusted recipes. As a sodden November turned into an even more sodden December, he was busy making four English Christmas cakes: one for us, one for our neighbour Francisco and his family, one for our dear Portuguese friend Mafalda, and lastly one for Craig's school Christmas raffle, which was to take place at the Christmas Fair on the last day of term. We were both looking forward to seeing what impact our cake made, as it was very different to the Portuguese Christmas cake which is called a Bolo Rei. This magnificent looking cake is made from a dough mixture, enriched with dried fruits and nuts, the top is decorated with big slices of crystallized fruit. The taste is often a bit dry and disappointing, although we had only tried one that we bought from the supermarket.

When we arrived at the fair, we couldn't see our cake anywhere, one of the teachers drew us aside and guiltily told us that our cake had not made it to the raffle – the teachers couldn't resist trying it, so they cut it into pieces and priced it up per slice instead. Once they had tasted the cake, they proceeded to buy most of the slices themselves before the Christmas Fair was even opened. They all looked bloated and guilty; and tried to humour us by saying it was the best cake they had ever tasted!

Mafalda was also thrilled with her cake, she gave us both little gifts, but for Craig, she had crocheted a lovely brightly coloured blanket, which to her joy, he was genuinely pleased with.

The last of the cakes Steve took along to Francisco and his family. Maria answered the door dressed in black, took the cake with barely a thank you and closed the door. Steve thought this behavior very odd, she was normally an expressive woman and he had steeled himself for a big bear hug. What could be wrong? Had we upset them in some way without knowing it? Our grasp of the language was improving but still not brilliant. We could happily talk about the weather, or the well being of their crops, but when it came to conversations about personal differences, we found it difficult with our limited vocabulary to express ourselves.

Later, Francisco came by to tell us that his wife's father had died. Of course, Steve remembered she had been dressed in black, no wonder she had seemed distant. They never mentioned the cake; perhaps they hadn't liked it and had fed it to the goats.

Christmas day dawned, Craig opened the presents we had bought him in the usual child like frenzy, then spent a happy morning playing 'Action Man'. The morning passed as normal for me, I travelled the 3k to the stables because the horses still needed feeding and mucking out. I don't think they would have been happy to have starved on Christmas day. Steve cooked a lovely Christmas dinner, I am so lucky to be married to a good cook, and after a few glasses of wine, I began to enter into the spirit. We sat around the fire opening gifts and reading letters of life back home.

One heartfelt message from Paul, who is my son and Steve's step-son, made us both shed a tear. He wrote that the time had come to tell Steve how much he appreciated and admired him for the way he had not only taken care of his physical welfare from the age of eight years old, but had stimulated him mentally as well.

We instantly forgave all the traumas of the past – especially the teenage years. Once, when Paul was about 16 years old, he came home drunk, crashed out on the sofa, and was sick all over my new carpet. Another time, after passing his driving test, he persuaded us to let him use our car while we were away on holiday for two weeks. He had four accidents. Luckily I had amended my insurance to cover him, and the accidents were all minor, like when he reversed down our driveway, and somehow managed to demolish our garden wall. He then built it back up jigsaw fashion, without any cement and hoped we wouldn't notice. The next windy day the whole lot fell down!

One day he came home with rings in his nose and a bleached blonde Mohican hairstyle. It looked terrible, but I suppose it could have been worse, it could have been pink with green stripes! Now he is a Park Ranger for the Brighton Downs, helping to promote wildlife and its habitats. He is full of enthusiasm for his work, and we are both very proud of him. He has a wonderful wife and two delightful sons.

Mella had given us her share of grief as well. Her first boyfriend, when she was only 16 years old, was a Mormon. We did not realize the full meaning of this at first; he was a lovely looking lad, they were in the same class at school, and were both very shy. Mella would come home from school swooning because she had caught his glance, and he had smiled at her. This went on for months before one of her friends arranged a blind date to put them both out of their misery.

From then on they had been inseparable. But after a while, Mella's behavior changed, she became secretive and uninterested in her own family. She spent more and more time at his house and on Sundays they would drive with his mother to a church 25 miles away. I thought all of this was very strange and one night we had a showdown. Mella and I had always been very close, and soon it all came spilling out. She wanted to marry the lad, and become a Mormon. She had been having lectures in the Mormon religion from two priests who visited the boy's house regularly, and had been going to a Mormon church on Sundays.

I was dumbfounded; from my perspective, my beautiful daughter had been indoctrinated by some persuasive priests whose belief was that they were on a higher plane, and when the end came, they would go to a better heaven than non-Mormons. She was blinded by the idea of a huge white wedding in a Mormon Church in Salt Lake City, America, where they would live.

After my initial hysterical ranting, Steve and I sat down with her, and talked and talked and talked. She still had many doubts about what the priests had told her. We begged her to talk to us as well as them, so that she had more knowledge on which to base her judgments. Gradually the relationship between them both became less intense. The boy went off to Salt Lake City, to stand around in shopping malls, and knock on people's doors trying to spread the word of the Mormons.

After a period of tears and grief, Mella returned to the happy teenager she had been before. The core of a good family is hard to break, but teenagers try very hard sometimes, and we still had to go through it one last time with Craig – reflective thoughts at Christmas time!

Craig had by now become very good friends with Jay and Mo, the two English boys he had met at last year's New Year's Eve Party. On Boxing Day we were invited to their house, along with a few other English people living in the area. One of them had bought her guitar along. People who knew her, told us we were in for a treat, because she didn't sing very often and that she had a wonderful voice. It was an understatement; she had one of the most crystal clear beautiful voices I have ever heard. She sang her way through sad plaintive folk songs, but as more alcohol reached her brain, the songs became louder and grittier, and we all joined in. I thoroughly enjoyed myself. I asked her why she didn't sing professionally, and she told me that she had sung in a punk band when she was younger, and seen the bad side of the music business. Now she preferred to bring up her daughter and sing for friends who appreciated her. Dennie was throwing another big party for New Year but we rather fancied spending our first New Year's Eve in our new home. Craig wanted to go to the party and be with his friends so Dennie said he could sleep over.

New Year's Eve was a fine clear night, with a full moon. Old folk say that the weather changes with the full moon, so maybe this beautiful clear night was a good omen. As we stood on our veranda, we could see reflections in the sparking water of the flooded fields below us. Although the rain had stopped, the river was still rising. We decided to don our wellies and go for a midnight stroll. We sloshed our way to the edge of the river; the speed and ferocity of the water was really daunting. It seemed to want to draw us in; I felt my body being drawn forward, as if hypnotized by its power. "Let's go back," I said suddenly drawing away, "it's frightening."

At home, we poured drinks and waited for the midnight bells to ring in the New Year. We were enjoying a romantic kiss under the full moon, reflecting on our happiness at being here, when the door was thrown open and Nuno and a group of young revellers poured in, brandishing bottles of whisky and home made fireworks. We all went out into the yard, and as the bells started chiming, the fireworks exploded with deafening bangs. After a few drinks, the revellers tired of the company of a couple of boring old farts, and went looking for a more lively party. The boring old farts went to bed!

New Year's Day it was raining again. A group of young people had booked the horses for what we called a 'fun session'. This was for people who had never been near - let alone on top of - a horse before. These sessions had proved popular with youth groups from the cities. I was certain that they would not turn up in this inclement weather, but sure enough bang on 2. 0'clock, a cavalcade of cars arrived and about 25 young people came pouring down the steps, all clad in Levi's and designer T-shirts (mainly white); they were so excited about riding a horse, how could I refuse them?

I glanced over at Smartie, Guv and Foxy, cozily standing in their stables. It began to dawn on them that they were the entertainers for the next two hours. The look of disbelief on their faces said it all! "Sorry guys and girls, time for work," I said as the group swarmed around them 'ooing and aahing', patting and stroking. The flashlights from the cameras lit up the dismal stables, as they all wanted to be photographed with their favourite horse.

To stay out of the rain, I gave a demonstration in the art of saddling and bridling. Afterwards anyone who wanted to try could have a go. I had never seen such a mass of knotted leather in my life, poor old Guv had the bit over his ears, Smartie had the reins wrapped around his nose, and little Foxy had her saddle on back to front! This would have been a good sketch for the TV show 'Generation Game' I thought.

Finally we were ready to brave the elements, I could think of no more diversions to keep us inside. Steve arrived on cue, to help me lead the three horses; he had the uncanny knack of always managing to miss out on the hassle of tacking up and arrived for the easy part of leading the horses around the school.

The first three people mounted with varying degrees of success onto the already soggy saddles. Foxy was small, and posed no problem for most fairly active people, Smartie was bigger, but no real problem, but Guv was huge. Steve had made a special mounting block for people to stand on to be able to reach the stirrup irons. Luckily Guv was a gentle giant and stood perfectly still whilst people clambered on board. The cameras clicked continuously as each group of three posed like cowboys on their mounts before the air filled with shrieks and screams as the horses lurched forward and plodded around the sodden school.

You always get a few people who think it's easy, and want to go faster. To be able to trot is not as easy as it looks, and after a few rounds of bouncing about, they were soon begging me to stop the horse for them!

The horses took it all in their stride, it was just another day for them. After the saddles and bridles had been removed the three of them had a roll of honour, they knew that this was their finale, and as they crumpled into the sand and rolled on their backs, plastering themselves in wet sand, the cameras clicked one last time before we all said our goodbyes.

Everyone had enjoyed themselves despite the fact that their designer T-shirts and spotless Levi's were now looking rather dishevelled! Two men booked to come again the following day for a 'proper lesson' and after feeding and drying off the horses, Steve and I argued all the way home as to who was first in the shower. He had just finished building a little wooden cubicle underneath the veranda, with a bucket above sitting on the veranda. The bucket had a hole in the bottom with a hose fitted which trailed down into the cubicle, where a shower head was fitted to the hose. A large kettle of water was boiled and tipped into the bucket which was topped up with cold water. You then had 4 minutes of bliss before the last few drips fell from the empty bucket.

Most nights, Steve and I went for a walk with the dogs; it was not uncommon for the cats to accompany us as well. This night two adults and five animals set off through the forest. The rain had cleared, there was no moon, the sky was black, illuminated by billions of stars. The eucalyptus trees stood like tall white ghosts, their bark hanging in long torn strips like rags around their ethereal trunks.

In our torchlight, the path ahead of us seemed to be moving. It was alive with large toads and spectacular black and yellow salamanders. The toads had large round faces with huge eyes that reminded me of E.T. Their strong bowed legs propelled them forwards with surprising speed, their instinct driving them onward in their lust to find a mate. The beam of our torch was of no consequence to them, they would not stop their march or change direction, it was us who had to hop and dodge between them! The salamanders were much shyer, their gaudy colouring gave them no camouflage; they either played dead or scuttled off into the undergrowth. On any mild wet night at the beginning of a year, you can see them migrating from their underground homes in the search for water to breed and lay their eggs.

Suddenly I heard another noise, a definite 'meow'; our own cats had gone off prowling into the night, and anyway this 'meow' came from a kitten. "I can't hear anything," said Steve, almost sticking his fingers in his ears! "Yes there it is again," I heard its plaintive cry. Next minute a tiny tabby kitten fell into step behind us, it followed us crying all the way home. I looked at Steve, "No," he said,

"Just a little drop of milk?" I begged.

"No!" came the reply as he shut the door firmly behind us.

The little kitten just sat outside the door and cried. In the middle of the night, I could bear it no longer, I got up from bed, and fed him some cat biscuits and milk, then finding him an old jumper to sleep on, I took him downstairs into one of the dirt floored rooms. He curled up contentedly and went to sleep. I climbed back into bed, and Steve opened his arms to warm my cold body. He had been offered two months work driving a taxi in Brighton, and had decided to take it. How I was going to miss him while he was away.

Next morning, I took the little kitten to the village, of course nobody knew or wanted him, so we were lumbered. Craig was happy, and cuddling him close he started his favourite game of naming the new animal! He had been getting plenty of practice since living in Portugal! He chose 'Gollum', he had been reading 'The Hobbit' and this kitten, with his huge green eyes and demanding nature reminded us of the little creature from the story. Our own cats would not accept him into the house, so I took him to the horses stables, he could live in the barn with the mice. I just hoped he would stay away from the road. Next time little Susanna and her dad visited to have a ride on Smartie, I noticed her playing with little Gollum, "I'm looking for a home for him" I sneakily mentioned. Little Susanna was jumping up and down pleading with her dad and cuddling Gollum tightly; he said he would have to ask his wife. I was pretty sure they would be back to take him home with them and sure enough - I was right.

Sam and Jacky were going away for a year at the end of February. They offered Steve a lift to England, and they also asked us to look after their two female cats whilst they were away. We could not refuse, there was nobody else to take them and Jacky loved them both so much, they were like pseudo babies to her. Before they went, Sam and some other English friends arranged to have an auction. Anyone could bring unwanted items to sell. He booked a local hall; apparently one of his many jobs in the past had been an auctioneer's assistant, so he knew the patter. It was going to be fun.

One thing I missed in Portugal was second hand goods, car boot sales, charity shops, auctions, even jumble sales. The Portuguese didn't seem to be interested in buying or selling second hand goods, but I loved a good rummage and an occasional bargain.

The day of the auction arrived. We had nothing to sell as we had sold or given away nearly all of our worldly goods before leaving England. The first thing I saw on arrival was a large mirror. It was 2'6" x 4', and looked new, a sort of Habitat style with a pine frame. It would look great in our large living room, especially if Steve could make a chunkier frame for it, to fit in with all our chunky beams and window frames. He was already delving through a box of books looking for any juicy Sci-fi. It was hard to get hold of English books here; they are too heavy to bring out by plane in any great number and we were both avid readers. I would read anything except Sci-fi. I also found some books for Craig. His Portuguese reading was now better than his English, which worried me a little, I was happy that he had picked up Portuguese so well but I really wanted him to be able to read and write in English as well. I found Roald Dahl's 'Charlie and the Chocolate Factory' ; hopefully that would put things to rights!

We came away from the auction with the mirror for only 11 euros. We also bought a small bedroom dresser, very old but serviceable, a huge terracotta pot, some other knick knacks, and lots of books, we had not even spent 30 euros. I bought a box of clothes for one euro, but after looking through, decided I didn't want them. A friend, who was driving to Morocco shortly, said she would take them with her. The Moroccans love to barter, and being a very poor country the people are happy to take clothing as payment for their own hand made goods. I asked her to try to get me some hand made leather bellows for my fire. Craig's English friends Jay and Mo, were at the auction, so we invited them home for the weekend. When they visited, the three boys all slept in the caravan that was parked only 10 metres from the house. We actually got more peace and quiet having three boys at home, than we did with just Craig alone!

Our electric fence had been a godsend. We erected it on a new piece of ground where the grass was lush and long. The horses' heads went down to attack the gourmet meal that lay all around them. Even Cigano seemed to be enjoying himself, but after only half an hour, he resumed his usual position, standing with his head low to the ground – what was wrong with him? Why couldn't he enjoy life like the others? He rarely ate all of the food in his bucket, or much hay at night, I had the feeling that something was wrong with him internally and that it was getting worse.

Over the next week, his appetite dropped away even more, his legs and sheath started to swell up, so I took him off the new grass, thinking it was too rich for him. We had heard of a specialist horse vet from Lisbon. I phoned her for advice. She spoke good English thankfully, and told me that she visited Coimbra every Tuesday, which happened to be the next day. She was willing to make the journey from Coimbra to see us the following morning.

Her name was Paula; she was petite, attractive, and very young. She told us she had trained at Newmarket, and had married an Englishman; they were now settled in Lisbon. She thought the main problem with Ciggy was irreversible worm damage caused through years of neglect; there was also a problem with his lymphatic system. Cigano needed antibiotics daily; we would have to administer them ourselves.

Paula was going to have to give us a crash course in basic veterinary skills. I am no nurse, and couldn't imagine myself plunging needles into poor Cigano's neck, but Paula showed me how to fill the vial, and helped me find the right spot, then stood by expectantly for me to give the injection. I forced my arm forward towards the spot, but as it neared, it jerked away all by itself! I tried again, but had the same reaction. If I could have closed my eyes it would have been easier, but of course I couldn't do that. Paula was sympathetic, but adamant that I must do it, so with a shaking hand and a dry mouth I plunged the needle into his skin. Cigano barely flinched, he stood perfectly still. He had to have two different injections, one on each side of his neck for five days. It was one thing doing it with Paula standing next to me, reassuring me that I had the right spot, but tomorrow I would be on my own.

I needn't have worried, I soon became a proficient nurse, the swellings seemed to be going down and I was hopeful for his recovery. Then I noticed a bag of fluid forming just below his chest; it grew to the size of a melon. When Paula arrived the following Tuesday, she seemed baffled by the fluid and put him back on antibiotics. If this failed she would have to take a blood test, but she warned that it would be expensive, so I was pleased when after a few days the fluid started going down. However, he was now having a problem with his bowels, maybe it was a result of all the antibiotics, which were now finished. I hoped that once his system returned to normal so would his bowels.

One Saturday morning we arrived at the stables as usual to give the horses their breakfast. All the heads were over their doors, ears pricked expectantly, except Cigano's That was nothing new as he rarely acknowledged my arrival, but would stand at the back of his stable until I had taken in his breakfast and left him alone. Only then would he come forward and almost begrudgingly pick through his food.

This morning I opened his door and a rush of panic swept through me. He was lying down in his stable and obviously in a bad way. I called for Steve and together we desperately tried to encourage him to get up, as it is bad, even fatal, for large animals to lie down for long periods – the weight being too much for their internal organs. Cigano made a few attempts to rise with our help but he couldn't do it. "We need more help," said Steve, and rushed off to get Sam who only lived 5 minutes away.

I began massaging his legs, talking quietly to him, trying to will him to live. Steve returned with Sam, and two friends who were staying with him. One was a farmer, used to handling large animals, and his wife, who was a riding instructor. The men rigged up a pulley with ropes from a beam in his stable; we needed Cigano to make one last effort to rise, so that they could get the rope around him. It all seemed impossible.

I decided to run to our nearest neighbour to call our vet Paula for advice, but as I left the stable Ciggy raised his head to me, as if he didn't want me to leave him. This was the one and only sign I ever had from him that he recognized or liked my presence. I felt drawn back and hesitated for a second, then I left. When I returned 10 minutes later, he was dead. I cried for him, and the finality of death. It was a big shock; he was the first dead horse I had seen.

The men were discussing what to do with the body. It was Saturday, and a holiday on Monday, we couldn't leave it until Tuesday. Sam knew a Portuguese man with a front loader machine, who could usually be found in the local bar. He went to look for him and returned half an hour later. Following behind him was a shiny new machine. The owner had a huge grin from ear to ear; it was his new toy and he was thrilled at the chance to try it out.

All the men gathered around the spot I had chosen for Ciggy's grave. They furrowed their brows and stroked their chins, arguing about how deep the hole should be. They agreed on three metres, and the machine made short work of digging it. Then, turning towards Ciggy's stable, the driver expertly positioned the machine outside his door. After tying ropes to poor Cigano's legs, they dragged him out. I watched through a blur of tears, my body numb; it was as if I was dreaming. We had only known Ciggy for seven months, but I will never forget him.

Jacky invited us up to their cottage for a barbecue to take my mind off of the morning's events. I loved their little cottage set about 600 metres above sea level, above most of the forests on the lower slopes. It faced west and from their garden you could watch the most glorious sunsets across the mountains, some peaked with snow. We sat drinking wine and eating sardines, but the sun took centre stage, filling us all with awe, as it sunk slowly behind the mountains, transforming the sky through a kaleidoscope of colour before darkness descended.

"Just another boring February day." Steve's voice broke the serenity. This had become his catch phrase to make the folks back home, who were still trudging through slush and snow, jealous! I reached for my sweatshirt, and moved a bit closer to the fire Sam had just built up. The nights were still fresh, but no one wanted to go inside so we stayed huddled around the fire until the first stars appeared.

We were trying to start a business, but we were under funded, which is always a mistake, life was going to be hard for the next few years, but how can you put a price on moments like these. The evening was even more poignant for us; Steve would be leaving for England for two months the following week.

As the week wore on we both fell into a depression. Steve was still working on the house right up until the day he left, trying to fill each waking hour. Adam had decided to buy another ruin to renovate, he asked us if he could stay in the caravan for a month or so whilst he looked around for a suitable project, we were now all sleeping in the cozy little bedroom in the house so the caravan was free. I agreed readily, I would welcome his company. Sunday, the dreaded day arrived. Steve was due to leave at 5 pm. I had four young girls coming for a riding lesson at midday, but my heart wasn't in it. When I arrived home at 2 pm. Sam, Jacky, and another couple, who were to travel with them, had already arrived. Jacky had her two cats with her that she was leaving with us, they were clawing and meowing in their cat basket. It was pandemonium: Steve had not even packed. We had no privacy in our last few precious hours together, as the house was full of people. Sam was eager to get underway, so we ate a hurried lunch and then they left.

It all happened so quickly; I was so unprepared that I burst into tears. Craig turned and gave me a hug. "We'll be all right Mum," he said, "I'll light the fire while you make a cup of tea." I had to smile through my tears; he was growing up so fast. On Monday morning Craig went to school as usual. School meals were excellent. He had soup every day followed by a plate of meat or fish with rice or potatoes and vegetables, followed by fruit. The cost was three euros a week! After school he attended a club where he did his homework. I picked him up at 6 pm. I had spent the day listless and miserable. I knew it was not necessary to cook a proper meal for Craig, he was happy with a boiled egg and soldiers or spaghetti with cheese. I didn't have much appetite but was trying to work up the enthusiasm to cook something, when Adam came over from the caravan with a huge fish concoction. It smelt delicious and suddenly I had an appetite. It tasted good, fish, topped with mashed potato and cheese – wow.

One Friday afternoon, when I picked Craig up from school in Góis, there was an excited buzz in the normally sleepy town. There was to be an art exhibition that weekend. Stalls were already being erected to house the paintings, although none were on show yet. There were to be some attractions for the children; a climbing wall, a roundabout for the little ones, and for the adults, a gyroscope which stood about three metres tall. It had three steel circles inside each other on separate pivot points, so the person strapped inside by their feet and waist, on the centre of gravity can spin his or her body spherically, including completely inverted. The whole thing packed away into a trailer. The owner of the gyroscope, was a young woman who had been travelling around seaside towns in Spain and Portugal, setting up on popular beaches or hiring herself out for exhibitions, discos and parties. Her stage name was 'Nightmare', and she certainly believed in living up to it!

We got chatting and she told me that she loved horses and had always wanted to ride one. She asked me to give her some lessons as she would be staying in town for a week or so. She was very fit and had excellent balance, so she learned incredibly quickly. Soon she asked me if we could ride out in the mountains. When I mentioned to Adam, who was still staying in our caravan, that an attractive girl was coming riding, he suddenly developed an interest in coming with us. He'd had a few lessons as a child, but was far from experienced.

Right from the start, I noticed a competitive chemistry between Adam and Nightmare. I was riding in front, and I could hear them talking animatedly behind me. We were only planning on riding for about an hour, and after trotting through an olive orchard, we turned uphill through a pine forest where we sometimes had a canter. I didn't want to canter on this day because neither of them were experienced enough. I told Nightmare to keep Smartie behind Adam who was riding Guv, where he would be quite happy to plod along quietly, but with a cheeky grin, she pulled Smartie out from behind Adam and overtaking me on Roxy as well, she kicked him into a flat out gallop. Adam and Guv gave chase. I tried to shout after Adam to stop, because horses love to race. Adam ignored me; or pretended not to hear, and galloped after Nightmare, which made Smartie go faster! With her limited experience, Nightmare had no chance of stopping Smartie herself – disaster loomed; what a nightmare.

Sure enough, the track split into two, and without a pilot in control, Smartie hesitated. The sudden deceleration was enough to unseat poor 'Nightmare' and she catapulted through the air landing heavily.

She lay motionless among the heather; Adam and I both jumped from our horses and tied them to trees, then knelt down beside her. I was really scared, my whole body was shaking, what should we do? Adam loosened her clothing; thank god I had insisted that she wore a hard hat even though it was hard to find one that fitted over her dreadlocks.

I saw her eyes flutter, she groaned, and regained conciseness. "Are you alright?" I cried. She was badly winded and couldn't talk, but after moving her arms and legs she nodded slowly. I was so relieved I could have wept. Smartie, who had found his way back to us, knew something was wrong; he stretched his neck forward to sniff at us as we all sat on the ground. "It wasn't his fault," 'Nightmare' said weakly, trying to stand up through a blur of stars still before her eyes, "I let go of the reins, and was just holding on to the saddle". We rested for another 10 minutes;

she said she wanted to get back on, which was very brave of her. We walked slowly home, and to my surprise she said she definitely wanted to learn more when her body, which was already stiffening up, had recovered.

During March the weather improved. It was very cold at night with early morning frosts, but by 11 am. it was hot enough to sunbathe. Being a real sun worshiper, I was sprawled out on the veranda one afternoon, when Maria, my neighbour, called by with baskets of oranges from her grove. The Portuguese never sunbathe; she was horrified, telling me I was risking my life and ageing my skin, it was absolutely imperative that we go inside, out of the sun. I followed her inside, and made her a cup of English tea, which she loved, but as soon as she had gone, I went back outside, although it did spoil my enjoyment knowing she was right.

Letters started arriving from Steve, he had visited some of our old friends and passed on all the latest gossip. But that was not all, I discovered a new talent of his – he was very romantic in print, and his letters became my lifeline. I arranged my days around the postman's visit, and wrote long dreamy replies. Something else I discovered during my time alone was that I enjoyed writing. I had never had the time or inclination to write in the past, now hours would pass while I mused over simple details that had happened that day.

I enjoyed telling Steve what Craig was up to, of the horses and other animals almost as much as if he had been sitting opposite me at the kitchen table. Occasionally he sent us little presents, such as some 'Beano' and 'Dandy' comics for Craig, and something romantic for me, like a pair of thermal socks complete with fleecy insoles for my wellies!

One day a parcel arrived addressed to Craig. I picked him up from school with the parcel waiting for him on the passenger seat. His eyes locked onto the parcel straight away. "Oh, it's for me." He cried excitedly. "Can I open it?"

"Of course you can," I said laughing as I started the car and drove towards home. I kept one eye on the road and one eye on Craig ripping open the parcel. "Dad's sent me a box of chocolates, oh lovely, and some chocolate animals." Sure enough a box of Thornton's truffle selection lay within the wrapping. I tried to reason with Craig. "Why would dad send you a box of Thornton's truffles? There must be a mistake, look inside for a letter." I started to panic as he popped the first delicious looking creamy concoction into his mouth. "I'm sure they are not for you Craig," I wailed, as the second one disappeared into his mouth. I tried to snatch the box from him with one hand, but he snatched it back, holding it out of my reach.

I could bear it no longer, I stopped the car in the middle of the road, and we had a full-on wrestling match. Goodness knows what anyone would have thought if they had seen us, but even worse, the chocolates were being squished in our tug of war! Craig was very ticklish; the time had come to play dirty. I tickled him in the ribs until he was immobilized by giggles. "Okay," he submitted, "let's look for a letter." We tore open the packaging, and there sure enough was a note which I read aloud. "Dear Craig, It's Mother's Day on Sunday, so I'm sending you these chocolates to give to Mum, there are a couple of chocolate animals for you, write soon, Love Dad." Smugly I tucked the truffles, or what was left of them, under my driver's seat for safety. Poor Craig was left with a pink chocolate pig, and a white mouse, each broken into tiny pieces!

CHAPTER 13

MY LOVE LIFE

A very short chapter..... I first met Steve when we were both fifteen years old. My friend Linda and I were dancing around our handbags at the Top Rank Suite in Brighton, as we did every Sunday night, when Steve and his friend approached us and asked us to dance. We danced all night and arranged to meet at the ice rink which was next to the dance hall, the following weekend.

Linda and I were stood up! I was gutted, Steve was my first proper date and I had told all my family about him, including my aunt and grandmother! I was not going to admit to being stood up so we both walked home from Brighton to Portslade which was about 6 miles. I told my family that I had enjoyed my evening and I think they believed me.

I had told Steve that I worked in a grocer's shop after school and one evening when I was leaving to cycle home, he was waiting outside. He asked me why I had stood him up. It turned out to have been a mistake on both our parts, I thought we were meeting outside the rink and he thought we were meeting inside. From then on we became inseparable, he was my first real love and we went out together for six months.

His family had applied and been accepted for emigration to Australia. This was in 1968 when the Australian government welcomed Europeans with open arms, and many British people went to find their pot of gold across the sea. The Australian government paid the fare for families to emigrate, Steve's Dad had only to pay £10 for each adult, children under 19 went free! They were to travel on the luxury cruise liner named 'Himalaya'. Steve was due to leave from Tilbury docks, with his family on 28th December on a journey that would take five weeks. Steve's Dad told him that if he had been a few months older (16) Steve could have made the decision not to go, but as he was still underage, he had no choice in the matter.

I can clearly remember our last few days together, I thought my world was coming to an end. Everything is so much more dramatic when you are a teenager, we both made wonderful pledges of lifelong, undying love. Little did we realize that it would be 13 years before we were to meet again. We did write to each other for a while, his letters were full of the wonderful adventure the journey had been, and how he was loving life in Australia. He told me how they had all bought streamers at the docks, which were long lines of coloured paper, which they threw from the decks, down onto the loved ones waiting and cheering them off. He said it was a real party atmosphere, which continued for the whole journey. Once the boat was three miles off shore, there were no licencing rules, so Steve and a few other teenagers made full use of being able to walk up to a bar and order a beer! There was also a swimming pool and a jukebox which played all the latest Tamla Motown, and other music from the era.

It all sounded so exciting that I felt lonely and a bit jealous at first, but of course at that young age, I recovered quickly, and was soon going to the disco with all my girlfriends and having a wonderful time. I had numerous boyfriends over the next year or so, but when I saw Michael, I knew instinctively that he was someone special. He was standing on the edge of the Top Rank dance floor (that place has a lot to answer for) with a friend. It had taken them two weeks to pluck up the courage to come over and talk to my best friend Linda and I. We had been watching them slyly as we danced around our handbags, but we acted startled when they asked us to dance. Oh, the joys of youth!

Michael asked my friend to dance, and I was left, smoldering, with his friend. At the end of the evening, the DJ played three smoochy records, Michael waited until the last one before asking me to dance; and so our relationship began.

We both knew this was going to be serious, and within three months he had proposed to me. I was 17 and working as a shorthand typist, and Michael was 18 and working as a trainee accountant. We married two years later, and were happy for a long time, we had two wonderful children Paul and Mella, but by our late twenties, we were drifting apart.

I broke the news to my parents that our marriage wasn't working any more, and that we had decided to separate. Their reaction was not quite what I had expected. I thought they would be angry, but instead they were strangely quiet. I thought this was the lull before the storm, until my mother cagily told me about a visit they had recently had from an old friend of mine. He had asked for my address; however they had believed that it would be in my best interests not to give it to him without discussing it with me.

I knew who this old friend was, and I felt a great weight lifted from my heavy heart. I had been thinking of him recently for the first time in years. I would sit on the back doorstep, looking up at the stars, wondering where he was and what he was doing. I think my inner self was calling to him, and now here was my mother saying his name. "Do you remember Steve?"

CHAPTER 14

THE BROWN BUCKET

While Steve was in England, he put an advert in a horse-riding magazine for 'back to nature horse riding holidays in Portugal'. To our amazement we had some response. A couple booked to come in May, I had under two months to work out some trails incorporating as much scenery as possible to make for a pleasant week's riding. Adam had a motorbike and knew the area well, he offered to take me out to explore, so we arranged a day. I already knew where I wanted to go, I had been there by road in the summer with Steve. It was a little village in the mountains called Cabreira, it had an old stone bridge over the river and a lovely spot for swimming with a grassy bank, ideal for a picnic. We had thought at the time that it could make a nice ride, if we could find an off road route.

The day Adam and I had arranged, dawned clear and sunny; his bike had refused to start, so we took his old car, an ancient Cortina called the 'brown bucket'. It was totally illegal and falling to bits. We would definitely have to stay on the tracks!

We zig zagged up the mountain, using tracks that I knew well as I had used these trails many times with the horses. The old car was only a little faster than the horses had been in climbing the steep slopes, and we successfully (only just) reached the top at almost 1000 metres. The views were panoramic; the air was filled with an ineffable sweetness from the flowering gorse and heather bushes which were intermingled with multitudes of spring flowers.

We were now on a ridge track and were starting to descend to the east, which would lead us down to the little village of Cabreira. This was virgin country for me; the tracks were all good, they zig-zagged down the mountain which would make it easier on the horses. We rounded a sharp bend, Adam had to do a three point turn to get the old Cortina around, and there facing us was the highest mountain in these parts called Trevim peak. It reached 1200 metres, with snow on its peak – awesome! Today though, we were heading downwards.

Lots of the track wound through a rich forest of oaks and chestnuts; sunlight arrowed through the branches of the trees. This warmth had tempted the young buds to gradually unfold; changing the colour of their winter canopy to a bright fresh green. The vivid green of the oaks really stood out from the duller grey/green leaves of the eucalyptus plantations. The horses and their riders would welcome the shade during the hotter months. There was definitely potential here for a very pleasant day's ride.

We arrived without mishap at the village. There was a beautiful swimming spot on the edge of the village where the river curved. In the past, the villagers had brought their olives to this spot and stored them in little stone sheds, which were still there. When the olives had all been harvested, they would have taken them to the olive mill which was close by on the banks of the river. We could see the broken old wooden water wheel which would have provided water for the grinding process. The whole place had a very 'olde world' charm. Also on the river bank was a mill for grinding maize into flour which was still in use.

The river water was crystal clear, it would make a perfect picnic spot for hot and hungry riders to take a dip before lunch. We could even use the little stone huts as changing rooms!

So far our explorations had uncovered an amazing ride and picnic spot, I was really hoping we could find a good route home when we noticed an old couple walking down the track towards us. They went towards the water mill used for grinding grain. We asked if they would mind if we watched the process of grinding their maize into flour. They seemed very happy at our interest and introduced themselves as Ida and Alfredo.

Alfredo was carrying a hessian sack of maize which he poured into a hopper on top of two huge round mill stones. There was a lever protruding from a slot in the floor, he pulled it and almost instantly the top stone started rumbling around. As the stone turned, a whittled wooden arm, no more than a thick twig, with a small wooden wheel attached to the outer end, bounced and skipped on the rough surface; as the wheel rolled around, this wooden arm, activated a little door at the bottom of the hopper. We were surprised to see that the grains of maize fell singly and disappeared down a hole in the centre of the stone. This continued for a long time with not much happening, after about 10 minutes, a very fine mist of flour started appearing at the outer edge of the stone and dropped down a wooden chute. You needed a lot of patience to grind flour in this way, it took about half an hour to make enough flour for a few loaves of bread!

We walked back up the track with them towards the 'brown bucket', Alfredo said they only lived around the corner and asked if we would like to share lunch with them. My tummy was rumbling, so we readily agreed. They proudly showed us around their plot of wonderfully fertile land, well irrigated by mountain springs which bubbled up forming clear pools of icy cold water. They had three goats, tethered on the hillside, browsing on grass and heather, and chickens in a coop with an old dog chained next to them. The dog looked well fed and friendly and as we approached Alfredo took off the chain so that the dog could run free for a bit.

Ida was a tiny, wiry woman with a brown weathered face, a quick smile, and the most beautiful green eyes. She was wearing the uniform of the mountains...a floral pinny, a brightly coloured scarf, and wellington boots. She was keen to show us her organic vegetables including the ubiquitous cabbage, which grows all year in Portugal, also Nabo which is a type of turnip, good for roasting, while the leaves are used in soups and served as a green vegetable.

During the winter months the old people in the mountain villages still collect chestnuts. Before the 1973 revolution, Portugal was a very poor country and chestnuts were used as a staple to grind into flour as well as a starch for soups and stews. Ida and Alfredo had a sack of ready peeled chestnuts in their cellar and as soon as I mentioned that I loved chestnuts, Ida filled a bag for us to take home. Alfredo had been making 'quejo fresco', which were little curd cheeses, from their goats' milk that morning. He wrapped up a couple and popped them on top of the bag of chestnuts for us to enjoy later.

I noticed he had an old 50cc motorbike in his shed with a vinyl cape type cover which the rider wore to keep off the worst of the weather. Most of the older generation could not drive, so these little bikes were their only transport. I had seen many older men using this type of vinyl cape, it attached to the handlebars of the bike and had a hole that you stuck your head through and hung down at the back. Alfredo climbed, nimbly for his years, onto the bike, and pulled on the cape, to model it for me. "But what would happen if you had a fall? With your head through the hole, you are joined to your bike". I asked, conjuring up horrible images in my mind. He demonstrated that most of the time, the rider didn't put the cape over his head - he held it in his teeth! It still kept most of the weather off. I had seen men riding like this many times, and now I knew why. They could keep dry without risking being decapitated. The bread man, who delivered to our house, had a bike just like this but with two huge wicker baskets, one each side, full of bread. He had a vinyl cape that covered the baskets as well.

We had a very pleasant simple lunch of olives, fresh bread and goat's cheese washed down with a delicious alcoholic drink called Jeropiga, which Ida told us she made by mixing grape juice with the lethal Aguardent. They seemed content in their little mountain hideaway, and together with their goats and chickens, olive trees and grape vines; they were poor, but more or less self-sufficient. They waved us off, saying that we were welcome to visit anytime. I had been really pleased by the way my Portuguese language had flowed, I had understood most of what the old couple had said, and I think they had understood me.

The return journey was slightly more hazardous to say the least! We had just started ascending the hill which snaked up ahead of us like a piece of discarded spaghetti, when an awful smell of burning rose up from the 'brown bucket'. The hand brake had stuck on. Adam tinkered underneath the car but could not release it, so he just carried on driving. I can remember that awful smell to this day. Eventually it released itself, but we now had another problem, the tracks had taken their toll on the exhaust pipe, which finally broke away at the back end.

Adam was reluctant to use the handbrake again, yet we were still travelling uphill. Suddenly he leapt from the car, grabbed a large stone and wedged it under the front wheel. I thought he was abandoning ship and was half way out of my door when he yelled at me to put my foot on the brake. I scrambled back in and reached one foot across to the brake pedal. With the tools he had in the boot, he somehow managed to fix the exhaust, but the track was rough and stony, and within a mile, he had to repeat the process all over again. I was sure we would be walking home; the car sounded on its last legs, it was begging to die. Adam just laughed, "It's got loads of life left in it yet," he said as the exhaust fell off completely! We had just made it to the crest of the hill; it was all downhill from now on.

The sound of a tank approaching was not uncommon to the people living in the little slate villages dotted around in the mountains, which was just as well because that was exactly what we sounded like. The logging trucks used these tracks regularly to reach the eucalyptus and pine plantations. Most of the trucks were Second World War, four-wheel drive, ex-British army trucks, their fronts shaped like a bulldog with a shaved off jaw! The windscreens had all smashed years ago, and very few of the loggers bothered with such things as exhausts, road tax or tests.

To my surprise we actually limped home. All the frightening driving had been worth it, I would definitely try out this forested and mountainous route with the horses. They would be a much quieter, more comfortable, and reliable mode of travel! We clocked the round trip on the speedometer (it actually worked) at 20 kilometres, which is a good distance, and although some of the going was very steep, up and downhill, the views would make it memorable, giving our guests a real feel of the green heart of Portugal.

On returning I had to wait at the stables because a local farmer had arranged to pick up some manure at 5.00pm. He was late arriving, and was determined to get his money's worth, jumping up and down on the muck in his trailer to enable him to stack a bit more in! It was 7.30 when he finally started up the tractor to drive out of our entrance gate, which was uphill. He had too much weight on board, and his tractor was not powerful enough to pull the trailer load up the hill. I assumed, that he would unload some, but no, he waved down a passing motorist, probably a relation, and disappeared leaving his tractor blocking my gateway. Half an hour later he returned with his friend driving a larger tractor that pulled him out in minutes. My stomach was rumbling with hunger, I would have killed for a beer, and all for the equivalent of 4 measly euros! On top of it all he said he didn't have any money at the moment, and would pay another time. It was hard to earn money in this country.

Craig and I were both missing Steve, and after a month of his absence I was feeling tired and lethargic. The weather was improving and the cobwebs around the ceiling of our house were emphasized by the spring sunshine. I threw myself out of my lethargy and into spring-cleaning. Once I got started I quite enjoyed seeing the transformation of a dusty, smoky house, having been warmed by wood fires all winter. After a few days everything looked clean, I finished off by giving the walls a coat of whitewash. Our first holidaymakers were arriving in less than six weeks, and I wanted to make a good impression. With this in mind, and the fact that I was itching to have a go on the back of Adam's motor bike, I asked him if he would mind doing some exploring with me as pillion, around another area that I had noticed looked suitable for a day's ride on horseback.

After studying Military maps of the area, we set off one cold sunny morning on the motorbike. I was wrapped up in numerous jumpers, a heavy coat and scarf, as well as a crash helmet. I didn't intend being cold. As soon as we turned off road it became obvious that I was going to be doing a lot of walking. The torrential winter rain had gushed down the soft tracks gouging gullies in some places, whilst in others the top surface had been washed away leaving exposed rocks. The combination of the two, plus the fact that some tracks were still wet and slippery, made for some hazardous skids!

I felt safer on two feet, plodding along behind as Adam manoeuvred the bike through this natural obstacle course. But once we got onto higher ground the track improved and I began to enjoy myself. We explored many tracks that just petered out or led to a terrace of cabbages! It was so much easier exploring on a bike than on horseback. To work out a 20-kilometre circular ride, we probably covered at least 40 kilometres, but eventually we worked out a wonderful route.

It passed through the authentic old slate mountain villages, of Aigra Nova and Aigra Velha, which had stood almost unchanged for hundreds of years. Some of the houses were not lived in and others were summer holiday homes. These old houses need to be lived in during the winter time to keep out the damp from the mountain air. I truly hope that these charming old villages do not become abandoned and will be cared for, so that future generations can enjoy the history of the mountains.

We descended into the village of Pena; goats grazed on the green pastures, their bells ringing out from around their necks. A beautiful Serra da Estrela mountain dog lay basking in the sunshine, supposedly on guard, but he didn't even raise his head as we slowly passed by. On the outskirts of the village was a huge old cherry tree next to a bubbling stream. (the stream I fell into on Christmas day!) It was a perfect spot for a picnic lunch – the horses could be tied under the cherry tree for shade, and the riders could free their feet from their riding boots, and cool them off in the stream. The Peneda mountain loomed ominously over us. I wouldn't fancy living beneath such a colossal mound of rock. Parts of it seemed to be suspended in mid-air, and had probably been that way for millennia, but if one day a massive boulder were to fall, it would crush the whole village.

On the way home, Adam realized he was short of petrol, neither of us had thought to bring any money. He stopped at a small petrol station, and told the guy who came out to serve us that he would pay him tomorrow. The guy just shrugged, it was as if it was the norm, no one pays for anything on time. When Steve first started buying building materials for the house, he found the same attitude. He liked to pay for things on time, but when he took money from his pocket to pay for a truck load of wood, the wood yard boss looked at him as if he was mad. "Amanhã, amanhã," he said, with a dismissive wave, and about six months later, a bill would arrive. The Portuguese were so laid back about money; I don't know how they survived!

I had enjoyed my day out; on the way home, I took off my helmet and let the wind rip through my hair, it felt wonderful. We passed some friends, who waved us down to stop for a beer, and later Adam invited them back and cooked us all a nice meal. He was leaving in a few days, I would miss his company, I felt a little apprehensive about living alone with Craig in the middle of a forest in a foreign country, but I had my dogs. Toby was a brilliant guard dog and a great comfort to me. Bica had a good loud bark, but she would be gone in a cloud of dust if anyone threatened her, and Boneca loved everybody, rolling over on her back in the hope of having her tummy tickled.

Time passed, it was only a few weeks until Steve would be home.... and our first guests arriving. I was feeling lonely and a little melancholy when the parents of a friend visited me. Their spontaneous reaction to the aura of our house shook me. When you live in a house day in and day out, it's easy to become unfocused, especially in the state of doom and gloom that I was feeling then. They marvelled at the wonderful woodland views as they stood on the veranda. They were in love with the house, I could see it on their faces. I had been there myself not so long ago, so it came as no surprise when they asked if I would consider selling. I knew they were in a position to make a good offer, and thoughts flashed momentarily through my head; we could sell up and move back to England. But move back to what? A house in suburbia, a nine-to-five job? I watched the river, glassy calm above the weir, helplessly tumbling over the rocks which were now becoming visible as the water level dropped from the winter floods. Only yesterday I had walked out across the weir, barefoot, feeling the cold water bubbling up from beneath my toes as it searched for channels through the round smooth rocks. Life here was hard, there was no doubting that, without electricity or water connected to the house, and very little chance of earning enough money to support our large family of animals and make improvements. Yet it was diverse and challenging; I didn't know what the future held, but I knew I wanted to stay.

The two female cats that Jacky had left with us, were giving me plenty of headaches. Misty, the elder one had been born at our house, her mother was a cat that Adam had adopted when he lived in our house. She was a placid cat and had settled quite well, but was petrified of the dogs and of our two male cats. Every evening, she would wait in our big olive tree for me to lift her down and take her to the refuge of our little bedroom, where she ate her meal and snuggled up in bed with Craig. She soon became his favourite cat, as she was so affectionate, desperately needing the love and attention he gave her at nights. In the morning, she would slip away, not returning until the evening. BB had become very independent as he grew and preferred to spend his nights hunting in the forest so that, at least, had worked out well. However, Misty's daughter, Tara, who had nursed B.B. when we had found him orphaned in the road, didn't remember him now, she spat wildly at all the animals. It was impossible for her to adjust to life here; she ran away.

Jacky's cottage was about six kilometres away, I thought Tara would try to return there, and sure enough that was where I found her. She was hungry so I caught her quite easily by bribing her with food; I brought her back to the house, and kept her inside. She took refuge in Craig's underwear drawer and refused to come out, hissing and spitting at him as he tried to find a clean pair of socks or pants! He had to wear gloves as protection from her claws as he fumbled for his clothes. No amount of coaxing would bring her out. I was going to have to physically drag her out, so wearing thick jumpers and gloves, I tried as gently as possible to pull her out, but she pulled back and fought like a wild cat. Once out, she leapt from my arms, managing to scratch at my face in the process, and hid behind some heavy furniture.

Over the next few days, she must have found some way of escaping, and I didn't expect to see her again, but she returned one evening and ate a meal. I thought the trauma was over, and allowed her out again – she never returned. She made her way back to her old home, and luckily was adopted by a Portuguese lady who lived close by to Jacky's cottage. Misty on the other hand, grew in courage and was soon boss of our house!

During early spring the fields owned by the villagers, below our house, had been left to grass. Two or three times a week Francisco, Maria and sometimes their grown up daughter Carolina, would walk down to the fields and scythe the long lush grass, tying it into large bundles and carrying it home on their heads to feed their animals. "Why don't you let the animals graze themselves and save all the hard work?" I asked Francisco. He explained that by keeping the animals inside on thick beds of bracken, which grew wild and plentiful under the pine trees, the animals provided them with excellent compost. If the animals were allowed to graze the land, which was always damp and soft because it was so close to the river, they would damage the grass by trampling it underfoot. By cutting it themselves in small patches at a time, they had a constant source of fresh grass to feed from February until May from under an acre of land. Of course it made sense, but personally I love the sight of grazing animals.

The second cut of grass was left to grow for hay, and at the beginning of May, there was a flurry of activity. Whole families, including reluctant children and bent over grannies, were down in the fields scything the long dry grass. In Portugal, every year by May, the ground is dry and the weather is hot; the grass only needed to be left for a day or two, they didn't even bother to turn it. Then it was forked onto huge plastic sheets and bashed with pitchforks, lifted into the air and bashed again, the seeds that have fallen are stored away ready for planting next year. The grass was tied up and carried home. For a couple of days we had a constant stream of people of all ages and sizes, passing our house with huge bundles of hay precariously balanced on their heads.

Next the tinkling of oxen bells filled the valley, heralding the ploughing of the fields for the maize crop. Most families or small groups of neighbours shared an ox and a donkey. The oxen plodded along the roads and tracks, pulling carts laden with manure, which was the year's worth of soiled bedding from the animal and chicken houses. This was offloaded by pitchfork into piles strategically placed across the field. The smell that wafted through every crack in our house that evening was healthy to say the least! The piles were then scattered, ready to be ploughed in.

Watching an ox, with its handler, plough a field was most therapeutic. The lumbering gait of these lovely gentle beasts with huge eyes and long lashes was so slow and peaceful. Francisco had the delightful habit of whistling long slow ballads whilst he worked. I felt fortunate to be watching the last generation of a now bygone age.

After tilling the land, the maize seeds were sown using a machine pulled by a donkey - or if you had no donkey, the wife! It's true, I have seen a wife with her strong shoulders encased in harness pulling the machine, whilst her husband pushed the handle and steered the lines. This year, the locals were dodging between showers and thunderstorms. "Why didn't you plant last week when the weather was more settled?" I asked Francisco. "Impossible," he replied, "The moon was not right."

All the farmers in this area believed strongly, as did their forefathers, in the lunar calendar. "But surely," I reasoned, "the wet weather will rot the new seed." He assured me that the seed was safe until it cracked from its shell. "How long will that take?" I asked, intrigued. "On the full moon when the weather changes." he replied with confidence. Amazingly he was right.

Alison and Gill were friends whom I used to ride with in the Brighton area, across the South Downs. They wrote to me asking if they could visit and I readily agreed; we had our first paying customers arriving in less than one month. My friends could be guinea pigs, helping me to get the horses fit, and to try out, and help me remember, the rides that I had found. It would be fun and give me confidence for my first paying guests. It would hardly look professional if the guide kept getting lost! Ali and Gill managed to book flights for two weeks' time.

Everything seemed to be happening at once; Steve was due to arrive home only days before my friends came. He had been working hard and managed to save some money. Unfortunately our old car had been letting me down, especially on very cold mornings, when it refused to get up and go before the midday sun warmed its cold heart. Second hand cars were at that time very expensive here, so Steve decided to buy a second hand diesel car in England, and drive it home. He arrived home at dawn after a 19-hour drive from mid France, where he had stayed over at Steve and Carrie's place for a night; he had set off early and driven through the rest of France, Spain and Portugal. He was exhausted; and ignoring my amorous advances, promptly fell into a deep sleep!

A few days later Ali and Gill arrived, the house was full of people and I was happy again. To top up my happiness, my daughter Mella wrote to say that she was coming to visit soon. My friends had a good week, boosting my confidence by proclaiming time and time again, how beautiful the area was and how great the rides were. They flattered Steve, who was cook for the week, (with a lot of help from Delia Smith!) And they helped to get frustrated Foxy pregnant.

Silver was courting Foxy with renewed passion; he would gently nibble her legs, slowly moving up under her belly, whinnying softly. Foxy loved his attentions, but as he mounted her, his wonky leg threw him off balance and he couldn't aim straight. Ali, who happened to be a nurse, took hold of Foxy's head collar. As Silver mounted her, she clinically and calmly told me to take hold of his enormous organ and aim it at its desired destination! I was shocked; I thought she was joking. "Get on with it!" she shouted, as he rose to the occasion. I gritted my teeth and grabbed hold of the misguided missile, and told Foxy to think of England, even though she was Portuguese. As I guided it in, I hoped with all my heart that he had succeeded in creating an heir, I didn't fancy doing that again.

I wrote the day down in my diary, and worked out the approximate date of our expected new arrival. 25th April. Boneca was also pregnant; Toby was to become a father at the grand old age of nine, or in doggy years, sixty-three.

All too soon our first guests Bertie and Susan arrived; it was what we had been dreaming about for the last couple of years - a riding holiday business of our own. I had been nervously filling my time with last minute jobs, while Steve was collecting the couple from Coimbra. I put on my biggest smile as they pulled up in our drive, and welcomed them as they got out of the car. Bertie was older than I expected, he later told me he was 69 years old. Steve led them over to the caravan where they were to stay for the week, and arranged a time for them to come over to the house for dinner. Steve had obviously been chatting to them on the journey and now he told me that Bertie was a top judge at horse shows, had hunted all his life and earned his living buying, selling and training horses. I felt intimidated by him, although his manner was friendly enough and his wife Susan was very nice, he was very definite about what he wanted from the holiday. He was obviously used to giving orders. He wanted a well schooled horse; no galloping (that would not please Roxy;) and he wanted to experience the mountains of Portugal by horseback. It wasn't that I couldn't provide all of those things , because I could, yet I felt my newfound confidence slipping away.

That night when we were alone, Steve tried to prop me up, reminding me that our horses were excellent, the scenery was diverse and different from most of England, and that he was a highly practiced (on my friends last week) chef of culinary excellence. He proved as always to be right. Bertie liked Guv, he is such a lovely, obedient horse, it would be hard to dislike him. Bertie carried a small retracting telescope, beautifully crafted in brass. Whenever we reached the top of a hill, he would stop Guv and dropping the reins, take out his telescope, and study the surrounding views. This drove Roxy crazy, he hated standing still when on a ride, so I just had to keep walking him in circles around the group until Bertie was satisfied that he had seen everything. Susan liked Smartie's willing nature, he was such a happy little horse, his ears were always pricked forward. He always gave the impression that he was enjoying himself as much as his rider. Susan commented that she preferred Smartie to her current horse back home. However they both abhorred Roxy's inflated ego. Bertie said he would like the chance to 'straighten him out', and that he was like a spoiled child. The quote of the week from him to me was, "My dear, if you spoiled your husband the way you spoil that horse, he would be a very lucky chap!" I don't think he was being complimentary!

One morning, I found Bertie in Guv's stable, standing at his shoulder and dangling a crystal on a piece of string. Guv had an over active sweat gland on his neck, it was about the size of a smart phone and caused him to sweat just from this one spot, constantly. I always thought it was a leftover symptom of his stressful racing days, it had been there ever since I had known him, and it didn't seem to bother him. Bertie continued to stand with Guv for about 10 minutes each day waving the crystal over his neck. The sweat gland continued to sweat.

We enjoyed their company and they ate with us every evening, praising Steve's gastronomic skills, which ranged from aromatic Piri Piri Chicken, to fresh fish from the fish van that passed our house twice a week, Steve tried to cook from Portuguese recipes as far as possible; Bertie and Susan really enjoyed his Chamfana, which is goat cutlets, supplied by our neighbour, cooked in red wine and herbs. We also enjoyed an array of delicious desserts, he really did put his heart and soul into his cooking, and all without electricity; I don't know how he did it! We had no fridge or freezer, he had to shop or buy from our neighbours on a daily basis. He also put on a spread at lunchtime, consisting of fresh bread which was delivered daily, local cheeses and smoked meats. Our neighbour Francisco provided us with his own smoked hams, and Maria his wife, made a delicious smoked sausage.

We sat up chatting and drinking wine late into the night by candlelight. On their last night, they treated us out for a meal. Bertie asked us to choose a restaurant; we chose 'O Burgo' in Lousã, we had been there on a couple of occasions and always had an excellent meal. It was situated below the tiny medieval castle of Lousã. We left home in the late afternoon as the sun was going down, because we wanted to walk around the castle grounds and also take a short hike up the valley following the mountain stream that filled a public swimming pool. The four of us set off, following a steep enchanted cleft in the mountains where ancient trees, ferns and mosses together with wild flowers, grew in abundance; a true fairy paradise. There were places where the sun never reached and the rocky path became treacherous as we climbed higher. We decided to turn back; I didn't want to be eating supper with wet feet! We crossed a little footbridge over to the restaurant and sat at a table overlooking the water, which flowed through the pool and cascaded on down the mountains.

The interior of the restaurant was very appealing with gentle lighting and Portuguese memorabilia adorning the walls and shelves. Firstly we were brought a tray of aperitifs which included chouriço, black pudding, chick peas with spring onions and olive oil, also tiny goat's cheeses, tiny pieces of fried fish, olives, and a bowl of mixed beans in a tasty tomato sauce. We all sampled little pieces of everything, trying to leave enough room for more courses to come.

For the main courses, Bertie ordered a whole round loaf of broa bread which is a heavy corn bread, the middle had been cored out and filled with a stew and topped with lots of cabbage. We tried to change his mind as we had eaten this before, and found it incredibly heavy and the meat fatty, but he insisted that he wanted to eat authentic Portuguese food. It was definitely authentic, and probably dated back to the time when impoverished families ate mainly the heavy corn bread (which Steve calls 'stone bread') and cabbage, with a little bit of whatever meat was available. Well, we did try to warn him!

Susan chose Cabrita which is roasted young goat which she described as tasty and tender, served with the most delicious looking roast potatoes and small cubes of broa bread tossed in a bowl of nabos (turnip) tops. Steve chose 'Javali' which is wild pig, and was a great favourite of his, it's much stronger tasting than pork - too gamey for me. I chose barbecued Bacalhau which is dried salted cod, I had developed a taste for this salted cod, especially when barbecued. When we first tried

Bacalhau, we were not impressed at all. I could understand that before transport, it was difficult to deliver fresh cod to the mountains, so it was dried and salted as a preserving measure, but that was not a problem anymore, yet Bacalhau is still so popular all over Portugal. However I had developed a liking for the denser flesh and salty flavour, especially when barbecued. It was served with salad and batatas ao murro, which translates as 'small potatoes baked in the oven and smashed with a fist'! How could I not try those?

We couldn't decide what to have for dessert, so our waiter suggested he bring us a sample of everything. A tray of twelve small bowls was brought to our table, and we all enjoyed sampling a little of each. What a great idea. All of this food was accompanied by a couple of bottles of Vinho Verde, a fresh young white wine with a slight sparkle. The moon was rising high in the sky by the time we left the restaurant, our first week of work had been a great success. This was a very pleasant way to earn a living, and I looked forward to the next two couples (4 people) that were arriving in three weeks' time.

Albino, the man who had taken us to meet our first farrier, had become a good friend. He often rode his beautiful stallion Samorim from Arganil, where he lived, over to us at Quinta da Ribeira. It was a distance of about 25 kilometres round trip, but the horse was young and strong. Steve and I sometimes rode half way home with him just for fun and because Albino liked to ride Guv, and I absolutely loved riding Samorim, who was a stunning golden dun coloured pure bred Lusitano, with a long wavy black mane and tail. Albino had a Portuguese bullfighting saddle which was so comfortable; oh, I could have ridden that horse all day. Months ago I had mentioned to Albino, that four people wanted to come for a riding holiday, but I would have to turn them down because Cigano had died which meant I only had four riding horses including Foxy, which was one horse short as Tessie was too young and I needed a horse to lead on. He immediately suggested that I borrow his mare for a week. I was indebted to him; we could not afford to turn down the booking. His mare was a nice grey Lusitano named Roma., I had ridden her before and found her obedient and comfortable. I would have to offer Roma to one of the guests to ride, and although I didn't mind riding Foxy for a week, I would have to accelerate the process of getting her fit! I worked Roxy every day as well, hoping to quieten him down. I wasn't too worried about him because by mid June when the couples were due, the weather would be hot. He was always calmer in hot weather. I had warned the lady who had booked the holiday, that one horse was a bit difficult but she assured me it wouldn't be a problem, and that they were all experienced riders.

It's amazing how a letter or a telephone conversation can mislead one. From our conversations I was expecting a group of down to earth folk who would be prepared to muck in a little but when our second group of riders arrived, I had another case of foreboding. The two couples complete with matching cases, ultra trendy clothes and painted lips and toenails,(females!) alighted from their hire car into our rustic yard.

On the first day of riding, Rebecca, a beautiful girl with long blonde hair, refused to have anything to do with Smartie, except to ride him; she expected him to be tacked up and held steady for her to mount. She wouldn't even hold on to him in the yard for a minute in case he marked her T-shirt. Her partner, Rob, could hardly ride at all, suffered terrible hay fever when in the vicinity of any animal, and spent the whole week popping antihistamines and sneezing into his menthol paper hankies! He rode Guv, wearing gloves to avoid any contact, so when he wanted to blow his nose, which grew redder each day, we all had to stop whilst he removed his gloves and fished around for his handkerchief. Belinda, the woman who had booked the holiday, bragged about her riding skills, so I earmarked her for Roxy. I didn't like her, and either Roxy picked up on my vibes or he made up his own mind that this woman was not getting on his back. She took the reins very firmly and pulled them ridiculously short to mount him. He took offence and backed rapidly, threatening to rear and I knew he would if she tried to fight him, which she undoubtedly would.

I defused the situation by offering her Albino's mare Roma. Belinda's face lit up at the sight of Roma and she happily swapped. Belinda's husband, Martin, was small framed and lean, he had already decided that he was not riding Roxy, and was eyeing Foxy with much deliberation. He said he suffered with back problems, and would not be doing as much riding as the others. "She looks just right for me", he said, happily taking her reins and patting her kindly.

I got the impression that Belinda, the bossy one, had bludgeoned the other three into this holiday, and was determined to enjoy herself at the expense of the others. I had no idea why she chose us as her holiday destination, there were plenty of other places offering riding with hotel accommodation, which I would have thought would have been more up their street. At that time, we advertised our holidays as; 'Back to Nature

Riding Holidays', which was exactly what we offered. 'Bucket shower; compost toilet; gas lamps'; it was all in our brochure. Luckily however, Roma completely won her over, Belinda really enjoyed riding her and said she would definitely consider buying a Lusitano in the future. Martin, the little guy riding Foxy, was the nicest of the lot; he was friendly and very kind. He often got off and walked Foxy up steep hills, never complaining, and saying it was good for his back to walk a lot. They all loved the river, and spent most afternoons sunbathing and swimming. Luckily they all went out to eat every night, returning in loud drunken merriment, which went on until the early hours. They praised the restaurants highly, especially the prices! One local restaurateur later told me that Martin, who was the quietest of the group, had got up onto the table and almost done a striptease! The restaurateur thoroughly enjoyed it, and asked me when I would be sending some more crazy English people. They all wrote nice comments in our guest book, but I doubted we would be seeing them again.

One good point; I didn't have to worry about them knocking me up at 6.30am to go riding, as Bertie our first guest had done. "Come on girl," he would say. "Let's get out before the sun gets up." On hearing my muffled answer, he would shout, "you wouldn't last five minutes in Bertie's Belsen!" which his wife had told me was his groom's nickname for his own yard. I received a letter from Bertie and Susan thanking us for their holiday, they said that it had been a breath of fresh air to be immersed in nature and they were totally in love with Portugal. Bertie asked how Guv was, and if the sweat gland had cleared up. It hadn't, but I didn't have the heart to tell him, so I lied!

CHAPTER 15

SILVER'S SECRET

Boneca gave birth to three lovely puppies, two black and one black and brown. We named the first-born boy Hero, the little girl Pipocas (popcorn) and the little black and brown one, Odie, he reminded us of Odie, Garfield's sidekick. He had the strangest ears, which he seemed to have no control over. Normally they lay down neatly on either side of his head, but if he was startled or excited, they would shoot up above his head in all sorts of contorted angles, often actually crossing over each other on top of his head! He was a crazy pup and soon became our favourite.

Francisco wanted Hero, so when he was two months old, he came to take him away. Having six dogs at home was getting to be too much for me to tolerate, especially when they all went swimming and came galloping into the house shaking water everywhere! We decided that Bica, Boneca and Odie would have to go to Quinta da Ribeira, where the horses were kept, they would have plenty of freedom during the day, but would be locked in the hay barn at night. Toby and his favourite daughter Pipocas stayed at home, although I often took them to the stables with me when I was not too busy.

Boneca was worrying me. Her milk had dried up but she still appeared bloated, she seemed to be filling up with fluid. Steve took her to the vet early one evening, leaving Craig and I at the horse stables. The surgery was often busy but it was getting dark, and he had been gone for more than two hours. Craig, who had been making tea on our little camping stove, suddenly came running out of the barn. Something had really shaken him up. He didn't cry or shout, but his eyes were wide with fear. "There's someone asleep in the barn, I heard them snoring," he whispered.

We crept inside, holding on to one another in the gloom. Sure enough, coming from the attic was the wheezing sound of a 60-a-day smoker. Darkness had fallen, we had no electricity, and the wheezing noise from inside would rise to a crescendo then quieten; we were just about to make a run for it when I remembered about the owl living in the rafters.

Just then the headlights of our car appeared; we were so relieved to see Steve, but I was angry with him for leaving us there in the dark. "I suppose you have been to the bar for a beer," I snapped, but looking up into his face I saw sadness. Boneca had failing kidneys, the vet had drained five litres of fluid from the poor dog who, although much slimmer now, looked very weak.

Steve was intrigued by the wheezing sounds coming from the attic, he climbed up onto a big wooden box used for storing feed, then climbed on top of a door. Balancing there he could poke his head into the attic. I passed him a torch, and when the beam of light fell on the trespasser Steve fell silent and waved for me to come up beside him. With two of us tentatively perched on top of the door, I looked to where the torchlight fell. Two pairs of beady eyes glared inquisitively back at us from the faces of two, pure white, fluffy baby owls.

Barn owls make a vampire like screech as they fly through the night sky. I remembered hearing them when we had just arrived at Quinta da Ribeira and were living in the caravan. We were probably an annoying intrusion on the owls' territory. The first few times I heard their terrifying screech, as they flew low over our caravan, I felt shivers run down my spine.

The little chaps in the barn were probably half grown, about 12 inches high standing fully upright. With their fluffy chests puffed out and their heads twitching from side to side, they reminded me of a pair of Muppets! Through a porthole near the roof we spotted the white under belly and wings of the parent glide past. She was circling around the barn, obviously aware of our presence." Let's go and leave them in peace," Steve said, as we clumsily climbed down from our viewing gallery. "I wonder if that is the same owl who was living in the barn when Sara and Nikki were staying there"? I said.

"Probably", Steve agreed. "She could have been nesting in there for years, and never been disturbed...until now."

We took Boneca home to nurse her, but the fluid slowly returned even though she was on three different medicines to try to dry it up. She did not seem to be in pain and still ran and played with her pups. The vet warned us that she may have a heart attack because of the pressure, and one day while she was chasing Bica around the sand school, she collapsed. She was semi-conscious and breathing erratically, Steve said he wasn't going to take her to the vet, she was too weak; he would kill her there and then. I was horrified, but grateful to him, I knew it was the best thing for her.

I hid in the barn while Steve brought the claw hammer down on her skull. I sobbed as she yelped; I heard the second thud of the hammer, followed by silence. Steve was standing over her, hammer still in his hand and tears in his eyes. She had been his favourite; this was one of the hardest things he had ever had to do.

Throughout the summer we were kept busy by the children's holiday camp, which had come to us the previous summer. This year they planned to send us 300 children during the two months, bringing groups of ten at a time. They booked from 10am. until 12 noon each day. It was fairly easy work for the horses, who afterwards, retired to their stables to doze away the intense heat of the afternoon.

Craig spent most of his three month long summer holiday in the local town where all the youngsters gathered to swim. He spent his time diving, fishing, jumping from trees into the river, and playing with his Portuguese friends. He was totally integrated now, and had passed up to the next grade at school with a glowing report.

One evening I remember going looking for him at about 7.00pm. Many people were still swimming, but I couldn't find Craig. He was not playing football in the park either; I felt a twinge of worry. In England, I was nervous of letting him out of my sight for too long, but here it was different, I never worried about his safety. I asked a woman in charge of the changing rooms on the riverbank if she had seen Craig. She looked around calling her son to help. Other people heard and within minutes about twenty people were looking for him. One man had seen him riding his bicycle back towards the horse stables. There were two roads leading to the swimming spot from the stables, and whilst I had taken one, he had obviously taken the other.

I drove down the other route, and there he was happily cycling along in a world of his own! I was amazed at how everyone knew him and acted so quickly. On another occasion, Craig had a bicycle collision with another boy, his bike was hopelessly buckled; he couldn't even push it. He stood slightly injured with tears welling up; he didn't know what to do, but the owner of a shop rushed out to him and another man stopped his car and offered to bring him back to the quinta where I was working with the horses. The shop owner knew the car driver, so agreed. The man dropped Craig off at the quinta without waiting to be thanked, and the shop owner took the bike inside until I was able to pick it up. In Portugal they really care for their children, and look out for other people's children too!

My brother Richard, his wife Jean, and their children Tom and Emily, arrived for a week's holiday. Craig was so excited to be seeing his cousins again. We took them to some of the secluded swimming spots that we had found further up the mountain. Waterfalls cascaded into deep pools of clear water, often very deep and with overhanging craggy rocks that made great diving boards. Craig and his cousins spent nearly the whole week submerged in water. As my brother's family returned home to England, my daughter Mella arrived.

We were having a drink at a popular riverside bar in our local town, when our friend Nuno came and sat down beside us. I noticed the chemistry between Mella and Nuno was still there from her previous holiday. He was watching her intently, and she was meeting his gaze. Blonde, blue-eyed girls are not usually seen in these parts. I felt like a bit of a gooseberry! We finished our drinks and rose to say goodbye, I kissed him on both cheeks as is the custom and Mella went to follow, but as she leant towards him, he took her in his arms and kissed her on the mouth! I was shocked by his behavior, but noticed that Mella was not putting up much resistance! "Can we invite him to our barbecue tonight Mum?" she asked shyly. I had no choice; I don't think wild horses would have kept him away!

They were inseparable for the rest of her holiday, although they were slightly impeded because they had to take Craig with them everywhere to act as their interpreter. Nuno had become Craig's hero during the last year, Nuno could dive from the highest rock, climb the tallest tree, and was the fastest and most daring on his motorbike. He could catch fish with his bare hands, and light a fire with sticks; he was a real mountain man.

When we first moved into our house, we had a big problem with mice. They had already gnawed their way through a bag of organic wholemeal flour that I had been given in exchange for horse riding. One evening, when Nuno was around, we all heard a rustling. "Oh! the bloody mice are in the flour again!" exclaimed Steve. Nuno stalked across the room at high speed, he stood poised over the bag like an English Pointer dog, waiting for the next rustling. At the first sound, there was a blur of movement, a volcano of flour, and there stood Nuno with a cheesy grin, covered in flour, with a mouse already dead in his hand. "Next time I'll get two," he bragged.

A few days later, the scene was re-enacted; as Nuno stalked towards the rustling bag, Steve, who thought he had caught the mouse by chance, laughed as Nuno reminded him he would catch two this time. At the first sign from the mice, his hands were a blur, the volcano was bigger, and two dead mice were clutched in his hands. Then he said calmly, "Next time, three." Believe it or not, next time, he actually caught four, but one ran up his arm and jumped to freedom from his shoulder, so he literally did end up with three! After this we decided to throw away the flour, and let our cats take up residence inside our makeshift kitchen.

The summer drifted lazily on. Steve put a roof on the veranda, which gave welcome shade from the midday sun. He gave me a hammock for my birthday, stretching it out under the eaves of the veranda, I loved to laze in the hammock and be swayed gently by the warm breeze, listening to Francisco whistling while he worked in his field below. The problem was, there were always people staying, and it became tactical warfare as to who got there first.

Paul, my eldest son, arrived one day unannounced. Paul loved to surprise me, I had no idea he was coming. He had planned to hire a car, but on the aeroplane, he overheard an Englishman talking about Coimbra, saying that his daughter worked there and lived in a village that Paul recognized as being near to us. Paul started chatting to him. "Do you know Steve and Sandra?" he asked, not really expecting him to know us.

"Yes, I do," said the man, "I went for a wonderful swim in the river below their house, while my wife went riding with Sandra; I was swimming for so long, they all got worried and came looking for me," he laughed.

He offered Paul a lift from the airport which he accepted gratefully. I recognized him immediately, Julian, the ardent swimmer, who had disappeared up river until after dark, causing his wife Sally, and us to worry so much that we went out searching for him by torchlight. I was glad he did not have his bathing trunks with him this time!

I wished the summer would never end, but half way through September, the weather cooled, Craig returned to a new year at school, and I had one lady booked in for a riding holiday. She was coming on her own, and was very keen to learn more about horses and riding. We had a very pleasant week, and she fell in love with Guv. (whose sweat gland had cleared up and never returned.) "I'm going to try to smuggle him home in my suitcase," she said sadly, as her week came to an end. "I think I would notice – his legs are too long!" I replied. She loved the pups too, and later sent a letter of thanks, asking how they were, and sending some photos of them that she had taken. Unfortunately I had to reply with sad news; both Odie and Pipocas developed the dreaded Parvovirus and they had died within a few days of each other. I was heartbroken. The vet had not recognized it as Parvo, which runs a similar course to Gastroenteritis, but is more deadly.

To add to my heartbreak, Silver, my lovely white stallion, was going downhill fast. He seemed to have aged dramatically; it was as though he were saying "I've had my fling, now I want peace." He was in pain with his knees and shoulder, even though he was on anti-inflammatory drugs. He had also become incontinent, because of this the flies pestered him mercilessly, they ate into his skin, I covered him in fly ointment and hung a chemical flytrap outside his stable, but still they attacked him.

We had found a vet called Rui, who knew a lot about horses but had not specialised in them at college. We did not live in a horsey area, in fact I hadn't seen another horse apart from Albino's two Lusitanos, so there was no demand for any specialist vets. We were right on the outskirts of Rui's area. He mainly dealt with farm animals, but he had come out to us when we needed help with Silver earlier in the year. He had aged him at about 30 years old, he said he had never seen teeth that old! Rui also told us that when Silver's time was up, he would come and administer the lethal dose. I knew that time was coming; but I needed to come to terms with it. By November the weather was cold, I didn't want him to endure another winter, and so eventually I plucked up the courage and arranged for Rui to call when he was next in our area.

I led Silver Moon to a patch of grass next to where we had planned his grave; he munched grass as Rui filled the huge syringe with a lethal overdose of anesthetic. I stood next to him with my arms around his neck, my body positioned so that he could not see the needle. My hold released as he sunk to the ground. He was at peace; I sat on the ground beside him closing his eyelids as his body stilled. He had taken his last secret to the grave with him, but I would find out soon enough!

CHAPTER 16

LAST NIGHT I FLEW

We heard of a farmer on the Portuguese/Spanish border who sold good quality hay cheaper than we could buy elsewhere. We arranged to pick up 500 bales for our winter supply. Our truck held between 150 and 160 bales, so we would need to do three trips. It was a three hour drive up there, with an hour or so to load, then three hours back and another hour to unload at home. The farmer and his family were extremely hospitable, insisting that we share their meal at lunchtime.

In Portugal lunch is definitely not a cheese and tomato sandwich. The meal always starts with soup, and on our first visit we had huge steaks with potatoes and salad; we were also obliged to take home a parcel of bread and goat's cheese, 'in case we were hungry on the journey home.' We set off feeling bloated and slightly tiddly because, of course, copious amounts of red wine must be drunk with every meal.

Another time we had Arroz de Marisco, which is seafood, meat and rice, similar to Paella, delicious. On the last journey we were treated to home made salamis, cold meats, and black pudding. The farmer's wife told us she used hardly any fat in the black pudding, just lashings of red wine and garlic. We loved the puddings so much she insisted we take home a couple that she had just made. The lunches were always very lively affairs, the farmer was Portuguese, his wife was French and their daughter was married to a Spaniard. There was also a smattering of English thrown in for our benefit. What a shame the horses could not eat more than 500 bales a year!

Steve was working on our kitchen, which was a dark, dirt floored room that would have housed animals in the past. He cautiously knocked large holes in the metre thick, ancient stone and mud walls, to make doors and windows. Sunlight invaded the darkness; he cleaned all the old oak beams on the ceiling, which were covered in years of dust and spiders; he rendered and whitewashed the walls, and concreted the floor ready for tiling. He built an oak recess in which he fitted our wood-burning stove.

The cost of buying the hay, and materials for the kitchen, had depleted our bank balance. Once again Steve started making plans to return to England to work for a while. He left at the end of November, and would be away over Christmas. I faced up to lonely days and endless games of Monopoly in the evenings with Craig. I had more friends here now and we had been invited out for Christmas dinner. Also, we had noticed that telephone poles had recently been erected along our road from the village, surely this meant that we were to be connected imminently? We tried to phone the company from the bar, but it was impossible to get through from a payphone. About a month passed and we were giving up hope, when two men arrived from the phone company and connected us....we were now on the phone! Yippee, this made a huge difference. At least now Steve and my family could phone regularly and I wouldn't feel so cut off.

One evening Mella phoned to say she was coming out for Christmas. It was the best present I could have had. Craig and I went to meet her from Coimbra, she was laden down with presents from all the family. We bought a Christmas tree from the local market, and surrounded it with parcels, illuminating it at night with a circle of candles. Mella did not want to get involved with Nuno again as she now had a boyfriend back home. However, one night as we were having drinks at a mutual friend's house, he appeared in the doorway. He slowly looked around the room until his eyes found hers. I could feel the electricity between them, and from then on they were together every day.

He should have been working, the Portuguese only celebrated Christmas Eve and Christmas Day, they didn't indulge in a two-week extravaganza of eating, drinking, and Alka Seltzer! I was worried he would be in trouble with his boss, but he was living for the moment, a true Latin lover. We all went walking in the mountains, he took us to places we had not known existed, huge caves with tunnels and hidden entrances; we smashed open rocks looking for crystals. He also chopped loads of wood for our fire; sometimes it comes in handy having a pretty daughter.

Nuno came with us to the bus station when the time came for Mella to leave. He had learnt some English and asked her to stay, he told her he loved her with tears in his eyes. She told him he fell in love too easily, and would soon forget her, but as she boarded the bus to Lisbon airport, I saw a tear glint in her eyes.

Spring arrived early; in fact by half way through January our house was in full sunshine until 4.00pm. Steve was back from England, and we spent a week or so luxuriating in each other's company. We enjoyed the warm sunshine and planned what to do next on our house. We were still living on the upper floor only. Our options were to build a set of stairs, linking the upstairs to the downstairs, and finish the kitchen, or we could start on the last room in the house, another dark dirt floored room, which we had planned to make our bedroom.

We decided to leave the bedroom until last. We were all happy and cosy sleeping in the little bedroom with its lovely four poster bed. Craig had a small bed at the bottom of ours usually shared with at least one cat, I will always remember waking in the mornings and him reliving his dreams of the night. One morning he sat up in bed and said "Last night I flew" . WOW!

We decided on finishing the kitchen, so Steve's first job would be to knock a double doorway in the south facing side of the kitchen to let the sun in. Any work on old stone houses is slow. The river boulders from which ours had been built were of all shapes and sizes. Once he had decided on the dimensions for the doorway, it was impossible to break or cut any boulders sticking out into the door space. Each one had to be carefully removed. Some were too big to lift and had to be rolled out, causing Steve to step smartly away as it crashed to the ground.

We had been told that the local railway station sometimes sold old solid oak railway sleepers. We were in luck and managed to buy one cheaply. It took three men to lift it into our horsebox, and after cutting to size and cleaning it up, it made an authentic lintel for the doorway. It looked strong enough to hold the house up on its own! Steve rebuilt the sides of the gaping cavity with smaller rocks and cement. Occasionally when we took out a large boulder, others would tumble out with it. the mud holding them having been washed away over the centuries. Mice caused another problem! They had dug out the mud in many places and filled it with anything soft to make themselves comfortable nests. These holes, though small on the outside, were like caverns inside. Steve would throw a handful of cement to fill a small hole, and end up using a whole wheelbarrow full, just as he had when building the veranda.

This episode in our home's renovation made us aware of how fragile the old house was, and how much it was in need of constant care. If Adam had not put a new roof on it, and we had not carried on with the renovations, how long would it have withstood nature's constant onslaught? How long before it would have slipped back into the river from whence it came?

Mafalda's youngest son Tiago, was a musician, he was going through a divorce and had moved back into his mother's house. He was converting her cellar, which was where all the wines would have been stored when Mafalda's farm was in full production, into an apartment for himself. Steve had become friendly with Tiago, and was helping him to clear out the cellar when he noticed two full sized, very old chestnut shutters. They were in the cellar awaiting the chop for firewood. "Burn these works of art?", Steve grimaced. "They have been hand made, and only need to be cleaned."

"Take them," said Tiago; "Come and see my new ones." The old shutters had been replaced by aluminium ones which were all the fashion here. Steve barely gave them a glance; he was already loading his new acquisitions onto the roof racks of our car!

Our kitchen was taking shape. We now had plenty of light from the original double doors on the north side, and the new doorway on the south, also the window that Steve had already put in on the eastern side, would let in the early morning sun. We would also get a lovely through breeze during the hot summer months. We planned to have glass doors to let in as much light as possible. Our 'new' shutters, now in place, would be closed for extra warmth in the winter. Steve had given the shutters a light planing to remove surface woodworm. There had been a bit of rot along the bottom, but as they were too long for our doorway, he had been able to cut it off. He coated them in linseed oil, which the wood drunk in greedily. We were thrilled with our new shutters, they looked fantastic and suited the house perfectly.

Our first bookings for trekking holidays for the year were trickling in. We had a lot of enquiries, but firm bookings were few and far between. After some thought, we decided that the main reason for this was our total lack of plumbing! Although most people were happy to sleep in a caravan, the idea of not having a bathroom was too hard to cope with. Steve's desire to hand build our kitchen cupboards would have to wait. We abandoned the kitchen and started plans for a bathroom.

One day Steve and Nuno were talking about the possibilities of hiring a machine to dig a hole for a septic tank. The problem was that there was no access for a machine. "Dig it by hand," Nuno the Muscleman suggested. Steve laughed at him. "Dig a ten foot square hole, through layers of rock, by hand?" Nuno shrugged. "Two men could do it in four hours," he said. "Okay, when can you start?" replied Steve.

Nuno was conveniently busy for the next few weeks, so Steve started digging alone. He tunnelled away for several days, until I couldn't see him at all. I could only hear the rhythmic sound of the shovel followed by the thud of discarded earth. He pick-axed his way through layers of rock until, at ten feet down; he met the water table and had to stop. The next time Nuno came around he was impressed. "How long did that take you?" he asked. "Oh, about four hours." Steve casually replied.

Francisco showed great interest in the hole. He was always setting traps for various animals. "What's it for?" he asked, peering down at the top of Steve's head, and wondering what the crazy Englishman was up to now. "It's an elephant trap," quipped Steve. Francisco frowned; he was never sure how to take Steve's sense of humour. After a while a little grin spread across his face. "Ah, it's a septic tank. I wouldn't do it like that; I would do it like this!

Francisco came by every day to inspect the progress of the tank. In his opinion, nothing Steve did was right; it was not the way HE would have done it. Steve humoured him and carried on with his brick laying. He made a solid cement top with two inspection hatches. It was a very smart tank, Steve suggested throwing a 'septic tank' party – in the tank itself. Being claustrophobic, I declined.

The next step was to build a bathroom. We already had a bucket shower system under the veranda, so this was the obvious place to build it. It took about two weeks to build a nice brick bathroom. Steve had a window frame and door frame made at the local wood yard. He found a nice, old pine door in his wood shed that he'd scored from someone, somewhere! He stripped off the green paint - a horrible job - and hung the door. What we needed now, before we could tile the room, was the all-important plumbing. Steve is not a plumber and had been dreading this part. It took him a couple of weeks, and as many tanks of diesel in the car going to and from the plumbing merchants, to eventually get it right. At last we had a toilet that flushed; this was such an exciting phenomenon that we all had to have a go.

We had no mains water and relied on our spring for all our water needs. Luxuries such as a flushing toilet require a lot of water. We had a small ten-gallon tank on the veranda connected to the cistern by a hose. It was Steve's unenviable task to lug buckets from the spring up onto the veranda to keep the tank full.

Our new bathroom had a separate shower unit with hot water supplied from a homemade solar panel – an old airplane wing! The wing which had been lent by a friend was positioned on the veranda where it would be in the sun, then filled with water. Being long and flat, the water in the wing heated up quickly – as long as the sun was shining. If it was cloudy or raining, things got a bit chilly...so we kept our original bucket shower; which was a three-gallon bucket placed on the veranda, with a hole in the bottom and a piece of hose pushed through down into the shower below. You filled the bucket up with hot water from the kettle and topped it up with cold water, although the pressure was not brilliant, you could have a four-minute hot shower. It was important to remember the time limit and not daydream, as I often did. I have been caught out in mid-shampoo as the last trickle of water from the bucket brought me rudely back to reality. The airplane wing held a lot more water, so as long as the sun was shining, I could luxuriate in a long relaxing shower, but if the weather turned cold, at least I could have a short sharp bucket shower.

The sun shone all through the winter months. By the end of February the daffodils had come and gone and the trees were in full leaf. It was so warm that we often ate alfresco on the veranda. The abundant flowering of the mimosa trees enriched our view of the forest on the other side of the river. The whole landscape was cloaked in a bright yellow blossom, which mugged your senses with their sweet marzipan aroma.

Many of the tracks we rode the horses through were lined with mimosa; I liked to decorate the horses with the lovely yellow flowers. I would pick a sprig and attach it to their bridles. The horses were not so keen. Smartie was especially indignant, and would stand perfectly still while I attached the flowers to his bridle, then rub his bridle up and down his front leg until the flowers fell to the ground. Perhaps the colour didn't suit him!

Misty, the female cat that had been left with us and who now ruled the roost; presented us with two lovely kittens. Craig spent hours playing with them. He called one Night Rider, (his names were becoming more outlandish!) The other one was tortoiseshell just like her mother, who we often called Misty Moo, so Craig named her Moo 2. Sadly Sam and Jacky had split up and didn't come back to Portugal so Misty stayed with us, but the sweet little kittens needed new homes.

Foxy was heavily pregnant. I had doubled her feed and she was looking very well. Tessie however, was worrying me. Her stomach seemed to be expanding; yet her hip and backbone were starting to protrude. All the horses were wormed regularly, and she had plenty to eat for her size.

One day I was casually leaning over Tessie's back with my arms lazily dangling down on to her opposite side. I often stood like this as she had not been saddled or ridden yet, so feeling my weight across her back was good training for her. As I stood there chatting to a friend about the problem with Tessie's weight, I felt an enormous surge of movement pass from her belly to mine. Sure enough, I felt it again, a definite kicking. My mouth hung open, I was too shocked to speak, Old Silver's last secret was out; he had finally managed it on his own!

I worried that she was too young and too small to be pregnant by such a large stallion, I phoned my vet for reassurance. Luckily he gave it. "Don't worry," he said in his broken English, "these Portuguese ponies are very tough. She will be fine, just leave it to her." Nevertheless, I decided to bring both ponies home to our little plot of land so that I could keep an eye on them day and night.

CHAPTER 17

COMET AND APOLLO

We started operation 'Foal Watch' on 25th April which was Foxy's expected delivery date. We could see the ponies clearly from the verandah, and settled into a routine of shining the torch down on the field throughout the evening. Then, just before going to bed, we walked down to the field and checked Foxy for any signs of discomfort. First thing in the morning Steve would open the veranda and I would wait with bated breath. But each morning he said "No, not yet."

When Foxy's milk started to run from her teats we knew she must be close to foaling but we still had a couple of days to wait. At about 11.00 pm on 1st May, Steve was on 'foal watch'. He shone the torch from the veranda and reported that Foxy was lying down and that Tessie was trotting around. This was unusual behaviour. Then Steve said quite calmly "I think she's had it. I can see a dark shape on the ground." I don't know why, seeing as she was a week late, but I didn't believe him.

We both pulled on our boots and stumbled down to the field. Steve was ahead of me. "Yes, I can see it," he was saying. I was still muttering stupidly "It can't be, it can't be". Then I saw it too. All I can remember saying is "Oh, my God". It must have been only ten minutes old and was still lying down. Foxy was up on her feet. We had obviously disturbed her, poor girl. I just had to touch her foal. It was trying unsuccessfully to stand and we stood back to allow Foxy to help it.

Finally, it stood all wobbly and wet, when from nowhere, Tessie appeared, and deliberately knocked the little mite over. Foxy didn't try to protect her baby. There hadn't been time for her to lick it and trigger off her maternal instincts. She was only young herself and this was her first foal.

Our priority must be to catch Tessie who was coming in for a second attack. I couldn't understand why she was behaving like this, although I have heard since that this can happen when two young mares are left alone to foal. There is no matriarch to advise them as there would be in a herd situation. Tessie had become over excited by the strange smells and by this defenceless little creature that had been deposited on her territory. She had always had an aggressive streak and loved to chase dogs.

I should have foreseen that Tessoe could cause trouble but I assumed that Foxy, who had always been the boss out of the two of them, would be able to protect her own foal. Poor Foxy, she was so confused, but our priority had to be to catch Tessie. Catching an excited black pony in the dark was not easy, but finally we managed to corner and capture her. We tied her firmly to a tree and returned to Foxy.

She still had not attended to her foal who was standing shakily with all four legs splayed out. It was a little boy! We led Foxy to him and immediately she started licking him. We breathed a sigh of relief. The milk was jetting from her teats and the next few minutes were like watching a slapstick comedy.

Foxy wanted to lick the foal thoroughly all over. She was not very gentle and a couple of times she knocked him off balance in her vigorous attempts to clean him. We helped him off the ground and his little head went up into the air. He had caught a whiff of his mother's milk and took his first few steps in the direction of this delicious smell. But Foxy had not finished with him yet and as his instincts drove him towards her milk, she kept moving her back end away from him so that she could finish licking him! Once she was satisfied, she stood quietly and gently nudged his bottom towards her back end. I lifted his little head up under her belly and wiped a drop of milk across his lips. Within seconds he was nuzzling in the right area searching for that elusive teat. He was still so wobbly on his legs that I stood on the other side of him, sandwiching him between me and Foxy.

I am certain they would have managed without me but I wanted to be there. Foxy didn't mind in the least. She was nickering softly from time to time as if she was blissfully happy to be a mother. It was the year of the Hale Bop Comet, which had been high in the sky every night. We wanted a cosmic connection between this foal and his father, Silver Moon. It was a foregone conclusion - we would call him Comet.

I was so happy standing in the field as the midnight bells rang out. Little Comet was trying to suck my fingers. He was only an hour old but he was getting more and more confident at this walking business and looking less and less like the town drunk. He was already an expert at seeking out his mother's magic nipple and drinking the white gold that sprang from it. I was like a new mum myself. After the initial fear of the birth I felt elated and so full of love for this gawky little chap.

He formed a strong bond with Steve and I that night. "I hope he will always be with us." I said.

"Of course he will," Steve reassured, "He's special!" It was 2am and I was feeling very tired, Steve suggested I get myself off to bed. He decided to get a sleeping bag and bed down in the field to keep an eye on things. He made himself as comfortable as possible near Tessie, who would have to stay tied to the tree until morning. I gave both mares plenty of hay and went to bed.

I was up again at 6.00 am. Armed with a flask of hot water, soap and some antiseptic cream, I made my way down to the field. There was a heavy dew and poor Steve was cold and damp in his sleeping bag. He drowsily crawled up to the house for a couple of hours sleep in a warm bed. I set about washing Foxy down before the flies got to her. Comet was lying flat out and fast asleep. He showed no signs of waking even when I crouched over him and put a dab of antiseptic cream on his belly button which looked clean and healthy enough, but the cream would deter the flies.

Craig jumped up when I woke him with the news. He had slept through everything and now, not bothering to dress, he ran down to the field in his pyjamas. We watched as Craig and Comet stood looking at one another for a minute. Then Craig walked slowly forward with his hand outstretched. Comet took a step backwards and Craig went down on his haunches so that Comet was bigger than him. Comet came forward tentatively and sniffed his face, then he took his fingers into his mouth and began to suck them. We could hear Craig laughing. They were new friends in a relationship that could last until he was a grown man.

Comet was obviously going to be a laid back little chap. I sat down next to him and stroked him all over. He was so pretty. His colour was dark brown, almost black, but he had grey eyebrows, grey tips to his ears and grey hairs flecked throughout his coat. Most grey horses are born black as a form of camouflage. A white foal would be an easy target for predators. Comet was going to be grey, just like his father. He had a springy, short black curly mane and tail. When he awoke, he was totally at ease with me. He lifted his head and I gave him a cuddle. Then he laid his head in my lap and we stayed like that for about 15 minutes with me stroking his soft, velvety coat. Then hunger called and he clambered to his feet for a drink from mum.

I went to look for Foxy's afterbirth. It is important that it is delivered within a few hours of the birth. I found it and, after an examination to ensure it was intact and none had been left inside her, I put it in a bucket - breakfast for the dogs! I went back up to the house. By now Craig had gone to school and Steve to work. I was alone in our peaceful home and able to contemplate the new addition to our ever- growing family.

We had bought a little motor bike because when Steve was working, I still needed to go to the quinta to feed and look after the other horses. The roads were really quiet, you were more likely to see a donkey and cart or a slow moving tractor, so I quickly became confident on my little motor bike and enjoyed the experience.

Today I had been gone from home for less than two hours feeding and mucking out the horses, yet when I got home I noticed a change in little Comet; he was more alert and energetic and much more steady on his legs. When I walked towards the field carrying two buckets of pony nuts for the mares. Foxy neighed and trotted towards me. Comet, who had been lying down, leapt to his feet and cantered after her. She stopped abruptly where I had put down the bucket and lowered her head to eat. Comet was not so proficient at applying the brakes; he concertinaed into his mother's ample backside. Amazingly, he did not lose his balance or fall over as he would have done a few hours ago. He tossed his head and cantered round her in a circle. He was only 12 hours old and already he was a little show-off!

I erected our electric fence to split the field into two separate areas. Tessie could now safely be released from her tree. The horses were still together but the wire across the field stopped Tessie from hurting Comet.

Once the initial euphoria of the birth had worn off, worry set in. Foxy had run milk a few days prior to Comet's birth. I knew this meant she would have lost the colostrum so vital to give the new-born foal immunity to infection and disease. He had passed his first faeces, called meconium, and seemed to be in good health.

I phoned my vet to see if it was possible to get frozen colostrum, but he said it was not available. He advised us to keep a close eye on Comet and to phone him if there were any problems.

By day three I was certain he had not passed any faeces since that first day. I searched his field but found nothing. It was possible that an animal was eating it, as it would contain a high percentage of milk. I knew we had a few hedgehogs in the area, and there were bound to be water rats and voles living by the river. Comet was thriving and showed no signs of pain or colic. He was a very happy little fellow but I still felt concerned.

We decided it was better to be safe than sorry and rang our vet Rui to ask for a home visit. It takes him two hours by car to get to us so you can imagine how expensive it is to call him out. But, like small babies, foals can deteriorate very quickly and two of the biggest problems are diarrhoea and constipation. We couldn't take any risks with our precious little boy.

Rui gave Comet a clean bill of health and gave us a mild laxative for him, more I think to ease our minds than because he thought Comet needed it. He agreed that it was possible that an animal was eating the faeces. He also agreed with me that he would gradually change colour from black to grey. He would visit again in six months to give Comet his injections. He had a quick look at Tessie but thought she was nowhere near ready to foal. This upset me a little because I wanted Comet to have a playmate his own age. He continually pestered Foxy to play with him but all she wanted to do was eat!

Comet could now gallop, turn on a sixpence, buck and rear. He was an exhibitionist and would put on a show for any of the villagers who passed on their way to their fields. Horses were a new interest here, people had loved to see Foxy and Tessie, but little Comet was a new attraction - he was a star! Over the next few weeks we had visits from people we had not seen for months. They all came to see Comet.

One night, when Comet was four or five days old, the weather suddenly changed. Without warning, the temperature dropped and a strong wind picked up, bringing with it torrential rain. In the morning the ponies' field was a muddy swamp and little Comet stood shivering uncontrollably in the cold and wet. We had nice warm stables at the Quinta but moving them back there would be a major operation. Tessie would have to go too because she would fret terribly if left on her own.

With her foaling imminent, it would be very difficult to keep an eye on her round the clock.

Steve decided that the best thing to do would be to build a shelter right there in the field. He made a wooden frame and covered it with a red truck tarpaulin leant to us by a friend. The whole job took less than two hours. We put a bale of hay down for Comet to lie on and to encourage Foxy to stay with him. The flapping, red tarpaulin frightened her at first, but Comet was in there like a shot. He lay down and rolled in the hay. I sat in there with him, gently reassuring Foxy that the big red 'monster' was her friend. She soon came in, unable to resist a whole bale of hay! There they stayed, warm and dry. Poor Tessie had to make do with the shelter of a tree. We hoped the weather would change soon - after all it was May and we were in Portugal. The weather didn't change. It got worse and worse until it was just like the middle of an English winter.

One Friday morning I had a visit at home from a man from the Council. He said something about moving the horses out of the quinta. He wanted me to go with him so that he could explain, so I followed him there in our car. He said that the council wanted to use half of the land to build a horticultural centre. I always knew it was possible that we would lose some of the land one day. We had never managed to secure a formal contract for any of the land, which had always worried us. Despite many meetings with the President of the council we had only received a letter giving us permission to stay on a yearly basis.

We had invested quite a bit of money and a lot of time on this land. We had cleared it, put in wooden posts and wire fencing, and built a sand school. This took half the land - about 5 acres, the other half was cut off from ours by an electric fence which we had erected. He wanted me to take down the electric fence so that the tractor could start ploughing without delay. The man then said that they wanted to start clearing the brambles from our field. He wanted access first thing on Monday morning and asked me to ensure that all the horses were safely stabled by then.

On Monday morning at about 8.00 am we heard a shout from Carlos, our neighbour who was working in the field below our house. "Ola, ola, ola!" he was calling urgently. Steve opened the veranda door and looked out to see what all the excitement was about. There was Tessie standing with a little black foal, already on its feet. Once more we rushed down to the field. Our neighbour said it had not been born when he walked past about an hour ago. I tried to approach Tessie but she put her ears back and ushered her foal to the far side of the field. She made it quite clear that this was her baby and nobody was going to touch it. We could see that it was another little boy. He was still unsteady on his feet so we decided to let them be for a while.

We named our second foal Apollo. He certainly looked strong and healthy. We were standing looking at our beautiful foals when we heard another shout. It was the man from the council. I had promised to have the horses in their stables by 8.00 am. With all the excitement of our new-born foal I had quite forgotten. I apologised and went straight to the quinta to put the horses safely inside.

At the quinta, large, strange-looking machines were lumbering off low-loader lorries. They seemed a bit over the top to clear a few brambles! I asked what they were for and was told that the council were to look for water and build a well. There was already a lovely, old stone well on the land but they wanted a new deeper concrete one. I saw no reason to stay and watch them destroy 'our' land. The horses were happy in their stables and I had plenty to do at home.

On returning, I prepared some hot, soapy water to wash down Tessie. I caught her, tied her up and washed her. She hated it, fidgeting and throwing her ears back at me in anger. I managed to remove all the blood from her legs and tail. There were no signs that the birth had been difficult for her. She was perfectly alright. I was amazed how such a slightly built young mare could give birth to such a large foal. He was really quite different to Comet who was compact and solid. Apollo was slim with very fine, long legs and an elegant convex head; just like his father.

I tried to get within touching distance of Tessie's foal but he shrank from my hand and retreated to the other side of his mother. I leaned across her and touched him with the tips of my fingers. He felt so soft, I wanted to give him a big cuddle and welcome him into the world. But as my fingertips touched him, he bolted forward as if an electric shock has passed through him. Tessie was being so wary and aggressive towards me, that Apollo obviously took her behaviour to mean danger. She was still tied, so I released her and they both trotted to the far side of the field. I hoped that things would improve once her hormones had settled. It was a pity I could not build up that early trust with Apollo, as I had with Comet. I couldn't understand why she was behaving like this - so different to Foxy who was happy to share her foal with anyone. Yet

I was happy that mares and foals were all healthy and the weather had improved dramatically. Life was good.

CHAPTER 18

SMARTIE'S IN THE WELL

The land at the quinta had been totally trashed by the big machines driving across it all day, leaving huge gouges in the grassland. Thick mud was thrown up by heavy machinery as it trundled across the rain soaked land, leaving hardly any grass at all; it would take a long time to recover, and until then I needed to find some land to rent for the horses.

Dennie, my friend who owned the farm that we had first visited on New Year's Eve, and the mother of Craig's best friends, came to visit us to see the foals. We were discussing what had happened at the quinta, and she came up with an idea that might solve the problem. She had a lovely big field behind her house, the land didn't belong to her, but she knew the owner, and said she would speak to him about renting it to us.

A couple of days later she phoned to say yes, it was all arranged, we could take the horses there for as long as we needed to. She knew a bit about horses and was happy to keep an eye on them and top up the water trough. It was a lot more driving for me to go and look after them but I would not have to go everyday, as she was happy to take care of them on days that she was at home. We would just take the three older horses, the mares and foals would stay at home.

We started to plan our next move. The three of us had all enjoyed our ride from the Monastery to Góis, two years before; this ride would be about the same distance but in a completely new direction. It would be good to explore new tracks and possible rides for the future. We could have taken the horses in the horsebox, but we were all keen to explore.

The day of the big ride dawned, it was a stunning June morning, we made an early start as it was going to be hot by the afternoon. Wild flowers gently swayed in the soft morning breeze, birds were all busy collecting caterpillars and insects for their babies, the only other sound was the thump of hooves as we rode along the grassy tracks, Roxy was bucking on the spot and tossing his head in jubilation at being free after being stabled for almost a week. We had been happy at the the quinta, it was perfect for the horses, but now I wondered if we would ever return.

We rode over the hills, staying on tracks and keeping off the main roads. The first trauma happened as we entered a village with a very narrow cobbled street. The front doors of the houses opened directly onto the street, there was no pavement. An ox and cart was parked almost blocking the street, and we couldn't see an owner anywhere. The beautiful beast didn't mind us at all, he slowly turned his huge head which was topped with rather long curved horns towards us as we approached him from behind. All three horses slammed on the brakes!

After assessing the situation and with encouragement from Steve, Guv bravely passed the ox, swerving his body away from the horned head as much as he could in the narrow street. Next Craig tried to coax Smartie forward to follow Guv but he was having none of it! One look at those horns and he was backing down the street with poor Craig looking rather scared. I was behind him so I turned Roxy across the road so that Smart couldn't bolt away, Craig had the brilliant idea to turn Smartie around and back him past the beast. Amazingly it worked, I copied and did the same with Roxy and soon all three of us were trotting up the street; the ox stood staring at us with his lovely big sad brown eyes and long cream lashes, unaware of the drama he had almost caused.

We rode through woodland and another couple of little villages then came upon a football pitch in the middle of nowhere; it had obviously not been used for a while because the grass was lush. We thought it would be a good place to let the horses have a snack and for us to stretch our legs and eat our sandwiches.

Re-fuelled, we remounted and carried on; by now the sun was high in the sky, we were all hot, yet we had at least another hour to go. We set off along a grassy track and rounded a corner, where we came face to face with a big red disused fire truck. It looked as if it had been there for years, grass and brambles were growing around it, but it didn't have horns so we didn't think there was any danger! The track ran alongside a road, with an electricity pole on the edge of the track. Steve did not notice that the electricity pole had a metal stay, hidden by long grass, which came out onto the track. Alas, Guv caught his back leg in the metal stay and did what horses do very well; he panicked and reared up. Steve did well not to fall, but Smartie, sensing danger turned on the spot and galloped back the way we had come, with Craig clinging on. Guv freed himself, but if we tried to chase after Smartie he would think it was a race and go faster - what should we do? A horse in panic mode can be difficult to stop, all their training is forgotten, their instinct takes over, and in some cases, they bolt. To our amazement Craig managed to pull Smartie up and turn him back towards us. He had never really taken to riding...I wonder why! ...He could ride but preferred to be with his friends, skateboarding. When I asked him how he didn't fall he said "I closed my eyes and imagined I was Smartie. I whispered Whoa, whoa, whoa and he stopped." He could be a good little rider if he had the inclination.

I wished I knew more about horse psychology. Why couldn't Roxy be friendly to other horses? If only I could talk to him - reassure him that it's okay to be nice. Why did Smartie shy at a rock or a tree stump yet didn't bat an eye when a juggernaut trundled past him? Maybe it was for the best that they couldn't answer back, we might hear too many things that they didn't like about us!

Finally we were walking through the steep cobbled street of Fonte Longa, and the field we were heading for was within our view. Everyone had heard that the horses were coming to their village, curious adults and children came out of their houses to greet us. They were full of questions, wanting to know what they ate; where would they sleep; could they stroke them and would they bite? We wanted to be on our way, my bottom was beginning to feel numb after three hours in the saddle. I felt like the pied piper as the chattering children followed us down the cobbled street.

At the bottom of the village, journey's end lay green and waiting, the long green grass swayed gently in the breeze. Once safely in the field, we took off their tack and let them go. In unison their three heads went down, they didn't even bother to roll or look for water after their long journey, they just ripped mouthful after mouthful of sweet grass. Dennie had owned ponies in her childhood but after a nasty fall and an incident where a horse turned and attacked her, she had lost her confidence and had not ridden since. Over the next few weeks, Guv was to give her back her confidence in horses and she was to repay him in a way none of us could have foreseen.

Dennie and her family owned a large rambling farmhouse which dated back to the 17th century. It was a grand house, probably built for the principal landowner of the valley. The quality of the stonework and wood joinery were quite amazing when you consider it was all crafted by hand. The farm fell into disrepair during the 20th century and had not been lived in for many years, before Dennie and her family bought it, and breathed life back into its forgotten walls. It had stables that probably had not housed livestock for more than a hundred years, yet as with the house, everything had been built to last. Massive 10 inch thick beams supported the roof of the stables, the walls were 2 foot thick providing a cool dark refuge for animals from the scorching sun and troublesome flies. Our horses would really appreciate these stables in the hottest parts of the day. Dennie had an old bath tub that we were going to use as a water trough, we dragged it out into the field and fixed a hose pipe up from Dennie's tap. From there it would be easy to fill the bath each day. We stored away the horse tack in a lock up shed and I told Dennie that I would bring over the horse rugs another time, just in case the weather turned wet. She asked us if we would like to stay for supper, and afterwards, she would give us a lift home, which we accepted happily. We spent a nice early evening just sitting in the field with the horses; there was no wind and the bees and butterflies were still hard at work. The three boys were messing about in a nearby pond, trying in vain to catch newts. Sheep grazed in the opposite field. There was an aura of peace enfolding the valley.

A Dutch family had bought a ruin just below Sam and Jacky's little cottage in the mountains. The family came to visit us to introduce themselves and also to offer Steve some building work. Hendrik was a rather fearsome giant of a man with a bushy beard and booming voice yet his eyes were kind and his manner friendly. He was the type of person who said exactly what he thought, things were either black or white to Hendrik: nothing in between. His wife Johanna was very pleasant, she asked Craig if he would introduce her children to our animals.

We had a nice afternoon in their company, they were enchanted by the foals; the children loved Misty's little kittens and Johanna asked me if her children could take one each when they moved over in a couple of months' time. She thought it would help the children to look forward to their new life knowing there was a kitten each awaiting them. It was a good idea, the children were so happy and so was I because I really didn't want to keep the kittens. I was also happy because if Steve had local work he would not have to go back to England for a long while.

Steve started work the following week, it meant that our own house renovations would be yet again put on hold, but we needed money to be able to move forward. We were now saving for a solar system so that we could have electricity at last.

Hendrik also employed another English man called Critter: he was a real hard biker type with a shaved head, steely blue eyes and tattoos and piercings all over - as far as I could see! He turned up for work each day on his Triumph Bonneville with half a dozen beers and a huge round loaf of bread, filled with chourico, cheese, and ham. He started eating as soon as he arrived at work, and finished just before he left to go home for the day. He was a real character and despite his appearance, he wouldn't hurt a fly. He was always recounting unusual tales of his life which kept Steve amused all day.

I bumped into Francisco in the local supermarket; I was still feeling down about the way we had been treated by the council at the quinta, and also worried that the mares and foals had nowhere to go; our little field was now completely bare of grass, and hay was in short supply. I had fenced off a piece of land at the quinta, and had been looking forward to taking them all there in a few weeks. That was now completely out of the question. Francisco asked me what was wrong, and soon I was pouring out the whole story to him, others in the supermarket crowded around to listen as I explained in my poor Portuguese. Many of the locals had come to visit the foals and they all listened to my tale of woe with sympathy telling me not to worry, they would all look out for land for us. That evening I had a phone call from the father of Ines, one of my pupils. I told him I was sorry but his daughter would not be able to ride with me for a while, because we had moved the horses away. I briefly explained what had happened; he said he had connections within the council and would try to find out what was happening. Then, just as we were climbing into bed that night, we heard the screech of brakes as a car drew into our yard rather fast, someone was running up the steps, and was at the door before Steve had time to pull on some trousers. It was a young Portuguese man whom we had not met before, he was rather the worse for alcohol which had probably helped to give him a little Dutch courage to visit us. He said he knew a man with a hectare of land nearby who was willing to rent it to us. We arranged to meet him and the owner of the field on Sunday. Our plight seemed to have touched the hearts of many people.

The field was very pretty, bordered with grapevines and some trees for shade, the owner walked us around the field, telling us that he was proud of the quality of his grapes when it dawned on me that horses eat grapevine! When I mentioned this to the owner he frowned, his grapes were very important to him, maybe he had been too hasty in offering us the field. I saw these thoughts going through his mind and before he could start to back out, I assured him that we had electric fence and I would make sure all his grapevines were protected. He hesitated but agreed.

What we hadn't taken into account was that because some of the grapevines had not been pruned and because horses have long necks especially for tasty bites of vine, we had to erect the electric fence 2 metres in from the edge of the field the whole way around. This just about halved the size of the field! Other than that it was perfect with a nice little stone barn which we could leave open for shelter. There was no water supply to the field, although the river was just 10 metres away, so I had to lug buckets from the river and fill up larger buckets which we placed in the field. Now we just had to move the mares and foals: how hard could that be?

We brought the horsebox down into our yard, and led the two ponies up into the yard from their field. The foals gambolled beside us. Tessie was being stubborn and would not go into the horsebox so Steve picked Apollo up and carried him up the ramp, she was horrified and followed up the ramp without faltering. Foxy walked calmly up the ramp and we assumed Comet would follow her, but he had other ideas. The grass in our yard was long and lush; Comet had never seen such grass before, he wanted to sample it. He skillfully dodged us as we tried to catch him - what fun he was having with these humans. He hadn't learnt to walk on a lead yet so there was only one thing for it, Steve would have to pick him up as he had Apollo. Comet was three weeks old by now and a solid little chap. Steve staggered up the ramp barely able to lift him from the ground! We quickly pushed up the ramp trapping him inside; and were ready to go. The new field was only two kilometres away.

Our field was stripped of grass, every time a shoot poked its head hopefully above the ground, it was picked off by eager teeth; this new field was lush, they were going to love it. On alighting from the box, the mares were eager to be released, yet inquisitive enough to do a lap of their boundaries with their foals skitting excitedly around them. They all trotted together like a proper little herd, Comet's little tail was held high in a proud stallion pose. He trotted ahead of his mother, with a beautiful elevated spring in his stride, he was the MAN of the herd!

Comet was still very affectionate and loved to be stroked and scratched. If I scratched his bottom he would curl up his top lip in ecstasy. He loved to lick my arms, legs, face, anywhere he could find bare skin, but he was starting to become too big for his boots. Once, when I called him, he came at full gallop, tail stuck up in the air. I put my hands up to stop him, but he kept on coming, rearing up right in front of me. On his hind legs he was as tall as me; I could not allow this to continue, he had to have respect. Instantaneously, as he reared up I kicked him hard on the shoulder, I was quite amazed at my own reaction, but I didn't regret it, not did I go to comfort him, I pointed my arm and with a stern voice I sent him away. He had to learn to be respectful of humans before he got any bigger.

One day the owner of the field arrived with a net sack full of lupin beans, he threw the sack into the river and tied it to a tree so that the river flowed over the sack. I was baffled and asked what he was doing. He replied in his very guttural accent that the lupins are poisonous to eat without being soaked so he left them in the river for a few days to soak in the fast flowing water. He warned me to make sure I only took water for the horses from upstream of the sack! Another day he arrived in a pick up van with the back full of dead bracken. He wanted me to bed the ponies on the bracken, adding a bit more each day but not mucking it out. I wasn't too sure, I didn't want them to start having problems with foot rot from standing on the soiled bedding but he assured me it would be fine. This was how he kept his goats and the soiled deep litter would be very useful to him as compost for his fields.

I started using his method and the bedding got higher and higher until the ponies who were a lot bigger than goats, were nearly touching the roof! Luckily they only went into the barn when the weather was very bad so it didn't affect their hooves, but I had to medicate them regularly because the bracken was full of ticks...Yuk.

Toby the dog was about to become a father again, it would be Bica's first litter. We had a call from the Dutch family who Steve was working for; they had already asked if they could take our kittens for their children, and when we told them that Bica was pregnant they immediately asked for first choice of 2 pups. They were coming out to check on their house in about another month and would call in to see the kittens, and also to see if the pups had been born yet.

Steve and Critter were working every day to have the house ready for Hendrik and his family. Craig and I enjoyed going over to Dennie's farm, he was now great friends with Jay and Mo, and it was nice for me to have someone to chat to. I had met a Portuguese couple who lived near Dennie, they asked if they could ride with me sometimes. They had both ridden in the past but not recently. Diogo knew the area well, so we planned an hour circular ride one evening. He led us through a pretty green valley bordered by grapevines, and on through a neglected apple orchard; across a shallow river and uphill through woodland; we were nearly home when we passed through a tiny, time worn village, that I had not seen from the road. It was more a cluster of about 6 cottages, half of them in ruins. There were a couple of old women, with deeply lined faces, completely dressed in black clothing, which was still customary in these parts, once the husband had died. A lot of older women still held with this tradition, and would dress in black for the rest of their lives to mourn their husband. These two old women were perched on milking stools and shelling a bowl of broad beans outside their cottages; we rode three abreast through the middle of the dirt road, but had to go into single file to pass them. They barely acknowledged us; deep in their own conversation. There was washing laid out to dry on the grass, and a small gaggle of geese honked in alarm as we passed by; thankfully they were behind a fence! It was an enchanting ride with the setting sun changing the colours of the landscape. I planned to explore the area more fully over the next few months, as Dennie was keen to ride, and so was another Englishman living in the area, but another disaster was just around the corner!

Another Dutch family had recently arrived and had bought a big farm in Arganil. I guess coming from such a flat land, Dutch people were drawn to this mountainous area. This family had brought their horses with them, and they asked us if we could arrange some hay from our supplier in the north. They didn't have a lorry so they asked Steve to pick it up for them. It was an early start, Steve was up at 6am. He had just put the coffee pot on, when the phone rang. It was Dennie saying that a horse was loose and could we come and help her catch it. I said I would be there in 15 minutes, I told Steve that I could manage without him, because we didn't want to let the Dutch family down.

When I arrived at Dennie's farm, an Englishman called Gavin who was briefly staying with her before journeying on south to Peniche to do some surfing, was already on the scene. Two Portuguese men were just setting off for work and hearing Roxy neighing constantly from the field came down to investigate.

Gavin had caught Guv, who had fallen three metres down into a stone walled rocky dried up river bed. He was trying to lead Guv, who appeared miraculously unhurt, downstream to where the wall had collapsed and Gavin would be able to lead him out. "Come on Guv, I'll soon have you out of here," he was saying, tugging on his headcollar. Guv would not leave; he walked a few steps, then tried to turn around. "Come on Guv, come on." But he would not go. I stood on top of the wall, I couldn't believe the size of the drop that Guv had fallen down. "Where's Smartie?" I cried. My throat went dry, my heart started thumping "Where is he? He would never go far from the other horses". Roxy was neighing from the field, Guv answered him - but where was Smartie?

I knew something terrible had happened to him. Suddenly one of the Portuguese men gave a shout "O cavalo no poço." – " Horse in the well" he was saying. We left Guv who immediately turned back towards the well, he had known all along where Smartie had been. We all stood around the top of the well, where the men were desperately cleaning away brambles; we peered down into the filthy dark water. And there he was, just his head was visible, his body completely submerged in thick muddy water. He was just touching the bottom which was a blessing, and he was alive. He was blowing through his nostrils in distress and obviously would have been very cold.

When he saw us he made a vain attempt to climb the sheer sided rock, but it was useless, he was 10 feet down a solid stone circular well which was about 15 feet in diameter. These wells are not usually very deep – probably about 15 feet, and this one was half empty already. The whole area around the top of the well, was thick with brambles, it took us a while to clear them away before we could get near enough to start knocking down the rock wall of the well. The two Portuguese men had gone back to their homes and collected tools, when they returned, they smashed into the rock with pick axes. They had the idea of pushing the rocks into the water so that Smartie had something to climb up. I was concerned that one might hit him on the head but there was no other option.

After about half an hour a section of wall was down low enough for Gavin to lean forward and attach ropes each side of Smarties head collar. Each time Smartie made an effort to get out, Gavin pulled on the ropes to help him, we all urged him with our voices, "Come on Smart." Obviously he had been struggling and thrashing about before we arrived, he was exhausted and cold, his body was shivering so much it was making ripples on the surface of the water. His efforts became less and less vigorous; he was giving up, his eyes were nearly closed. Gavin had lost his grip on the ropes and Smartie had moved his head away so that he could not reach them, I suddenly realised he was starting to float, his legs were leaving the ground, he was going to die. Someone had already called the fire brigade but we had to help him now, we couldn't wait. Suddenly I heard Gavin's voice; "I'm going in, I have a wetsuit, I'll be back in a minute." It was a cold grey morning, I forced myself to talk calmly to Smartie, over and over again telling him it was okay, he must hang on, we would get him out, but all I was thinking was that my beautiful little Arab was going to die.

Gavin came back complete with wetsuit and a big pair of army boots. He climbed into the dark soupy water and started pushing Smartie physically back onto his feet. Smartie showed signs of recognition that someone was trying to help him, his eyes opened slightly and he started snorting heavily again as he had been doing earlier. I think this is a form of shivering, his body had been submerged for a long time so he must have been freezing, shivering is a good response, helping to keep the blood moving and to warm the body. "Get some sugar," Gavin yelled, "It's an old gypsy remedy."

"Don't be stupid Gavin," I sobbed, "he won't want to eat at a time like this. I'm going to call the vet".

I woke our vet Rui, who had come out to check on Comet when he was born. He spoke English quite well; however being woken by a woman ranting in a foreign language about a horse in water was a bit confusing for the poor man! He didn't understand the word 'well' and I couldn't think of the Portuguese translation in my panic. He said it would take too long for him to get there and gave me the number of a vet from Coimbra. I phoned the number which was for an agricultural college but the phone just rang and rang. The college probably opened at 9am. I was not thinking clearly, I was in a dream, I wanted to be with Smart yet I was scared of watching the slow drawn out scenario, I didn't want to watch him die. Halfheartedly I searched Dennie's kitchen for sugar; I found some brown sugar and took it outside.

The Portuguese men by now had knocked a large portion of the well down, Gavin was tipping sugar, brought by someone else, down Smartie's throat. Most of it spilled out of the sides but he swallowed some. After three or four minutes the most amazing thing happened, Smartie had a sudden burst of energy. He thrashed up at the wall, the men grabbed his headcollar ropes and Gavin pushed him from behind. Smartie actually got his front legs, which were covered in blood, up onto the top of the broken down wall. He balanced there for a second, before sliding back into the water. His back legs seemed to be too heavy for him to lift. "The mud is very thick on the bottom," Gavin yelled, "It's holding him back. Don't worry, let him rest and we'll try again."

He started singing "Ding dong bell...Smartie's in the well!" as he massaged Smartie constantly. I couldn't believe his bad taste, I could have hit him! He was now pouring sugar down his throat for the second time, he was confident now that we were going to get him out. A few minutes after his sugar hit, and without any warning, Smartie seemed to have a last, massive burst of energy. We all pulled, pushed and shouted encouragement, and my lovely little Smart clambered free.

I couldn't believe it, I didn't know whether to laugh or cry. I didn't have time to think about it because he had to be kept moving to warm up and dry off. Someone ran and got loads of towels and we rubbed him vigorously to get his circulation going. Guv sniffed him all over whinnying softly, I think he knew how near to death his friend had been. Luckily I had brought all their rugs to Dennie's house so I piled two rugs on Smartie and Dennie gave him some porridge oats which he loved! I was so pleased to see him eating, surely this was a good sign.

His lovely slim white legs were a mess, yet as I studied his wounds more closely, I could find no serious deep cuts, just bad grazes, his head was badly marked but again, only grazes and surface cuts. I phoned the vet back to let him know what had happened, he genuinely sounded very happy for us but said we must look out for pneumonia. He said I must take his temperature regularly and keep him warm, he explained that Arabs were very highly strung animals by nature, this enabled their body to cope better with shock than a more placid animal. His body was used to coping with high stress levels, this certainly seemed to be the case as he was now enjoying some grass in Dennie's garden.

Once he was dry we put a new dry rug on him and turned him back into the field. Gavin and I went into the house, where Dennie was making coffee. The two Portuguese men left immediately for work on their 50cc motorbikes, they were wet and muddy and had probably gone without breakfast to help us. I was indebted to them and would thank them later.

It was a lucky coincidence that friends of ours, Sue and Rob, had visited us at our house the night before and after a few drinks, had stayed in our caravan overnight. Craig had been left alone asleep as Steve had gone to collect hay, and I had been called away in a hurry. I hadn't woken Sue or Rob when I left at 6 am, and there was no phone in the caravan, so they would have no idea where I had gone. Dennie had been ringing Craig at the house, periodically but had got no reply, he was obviously still asleep. Finally he answered the phone sounding very sleepy, Dennie told him that there had been a problem with the horses but everything was okay and to go and wake Sue and Rob and ask them to take him to school. He knew nothing of what had happened to his beloved Smartie, it was better not to tell him over the phone.

By the time I came in to drink my coffee it was all arranged that Sue and Rob would take Craig to school. I collapsed into an armchair; I had been kept going on adrenalin until now, I needed to talk about it over and over again. It was good to have Gavin and Dennie to relive it all with. A while later we went out to check on Smartie. He looked exhausted, his eyes were half closed, yet he was walking around aimlessly in circles stumbling badly. I didn't know what to do for the best, should he stay in the field and keep moving or would he be better in a stable? We all decided he should be in a stable; the flies were waking up and beginning to worry him. A neighbour of Dennie's had said I could buy some straw from her for a bed for him. The horses hadn't used the stables yet, so I had not bothered with bedding. I gratefully bought two bales of straw and made a lovely thick bed, then we brought all three horses into the stables.

I gave Smartie the biggest stable hoping to encourage him to lie down, it was lovely and cool in the barn, I put a quilted stable rug on him, then gave them all hay and water and closed the door. The barn had only one small window so it was almost dark inside, maybe this would help him rest. It occurred to us that we had not checked the field to see where the horses had escaped from. We found one small section of fencing down, maybe something had spooked them in the night and they had galloped blindly through the fencing and through the brambles, not seeing the huge drop into the well and stream bed. We were never likely to find out how or why it happened.

I went back into the house; Dennie was making toast, it smelt good and I ate a little but my stomach still felt queasy. I went to check on the patient, he was lying down on his deep straw bed, he looked such a mess, I started crying all over again, but they were tears of relief, he was such a tough little cookie.

I told Dennie I needed to go home for a bit and bring some supplies for the horses and collect Craig from school. She said she would check on Smartie every hour. Once alone in the car I kept drifting off into black thoughts. What would have happened if he had died? So many people loved him, his face, with half closed eyes was swimming before me as the tears welled up. I didn't want to be alone, so it was a relief to see Rob and Sue still at home. They were waiting to hear what had happened. They were regular riders of Guv and Smartie, both listened horrified as I told the story. I was eager to go through it all again, I just seemed to need to talk about it.

Once they left, my despondency returned, not just for the events of today but for everything else that was happening with the council at the quinta. I had to shake myself out of it, I would go and see my foals. My beautiful Smart was alive, I had been very lucky, everything else would resolve itself eventually, none of it seemed so important any more.

Over the next few days Smartie recovered completely except for the cuts on his legs and face, and extensive bruising on his legs He could not bear to have them touched but they had to be kept clean so I used another old remedy; I wrapped a layer of cotton wool around his legs then bound it with a stable bandage, quite tightly at the bottom but loose at the top. Next I poured warm salted water into the loose top of the bandage, a good two or three pints down each one until they were well soaked. The bandages stayed on for an hour or so until the scabs were soft and just fell off, and the wounds were well cleaned by the salt without me actually having to touch his legs at all.

Guv had a small cut on his front leg which did not seem to be healing too well. I hosed it thoroughly every day and applied creams to the surface, but five days after the accident, Guv's leg was definitely swollen, by evening it was much bigger. Next morning the swelling went from the top of his leg, right down to his hoof. I had never seen anything like it, you could have balanced an egg on the top of the swelling, his leg had doubled in size overnight.

I phoned my poor vet Rui, once again. I tried to explain, but he was just telling me to buy a certain cream, and it was too far for him to come. I knew he needed more than that, so I shouted "His leg is like an elephant's leg!"

"I am coming," came his reply. Rui was shocked at the extent of the swelling and said he would prefer to have him in a surgery but it just was not possible, there were no clinical facilities at that time within 200 kilometres.

He took out a large pair of tweezers and with me holding Guv's other leg up so that he couldn't fidget, and Dennie holding his head collar, the vet pushed the tweezers up inside the wound. He must have gone up about 6 inches looking for any foreign object, a thorn or even a nail that could have become embedded when he fell from the wall. He was also making a channel for the poison to escape, foul smelling discharge, oozed down Guv's leg, you could almost see the look of relief on his face, and although it must have been painful he hardly flinched through the whole operation. With a big smile the vet extracted an evil looking thorn; "Here is the culprit of all this mess!" he proclaimed. Next the vet squeezed antibiotic cream onto a lint swab and wrapping it into a 6inch long thin sausage he gently maneuvered it with the help of his tweezers, right up into the cavity. After applying an absorbent pad, the leg was bandaged to hold it securely in place. He gave Guv antibiotics by intravenous injection. Then he broke the news to us. "This procedure must be done three or four times during the next week, he must also have ten intramuscular injections a day for two days." I nearly passed out on the spot: he was expecting me to do it. "Obviously," he was saying "I cannot come every day to nurse him, it's too far and would cost you too much money, you must do it." I stood there mutely, then I heard Dennie's voice, "No problem - I can do it!" I felt relief gushing through me... she was a gem.

The following day we removed the outer bandage, there had been so much poison seeping out that it had pushed the antibiotic plug from the hole, which was already forming a skin. We knew we had to keep the hole open under all circumstances, so after sterilizing her tweezers, and with me holding up his other front leg, to stop him from fidgeting, she gently pushed into the hole as the vet had done, re-opening the channel. Guv stood quietly; as though he knew we were trying to help him. More yellow matter flowed out, she re-plugged the hole as the vet had showed us and bandaged him up again. Hopefully it would last two days.

Intramuscular injections are fairly safe to administer, but I am such a coward, it took all my nerve to plunge the needle into his neck. The vet had said he needed 50ml of antibiotics each day, but he wanted him to have it in 10 x 5ml doses five on one side of his neck and five on the other, rather than one 50ml shot. After two days poor Guv's neck looked like a pin cushion but his leg had gone down considerably. Dennie opened up the hole on three more occasions, gradually pushing the antibiotic plug up less and less, so that the wound healed from the inside out as the vet had instructed.

I could not thank Gavin enough, I am certain he and his gypsy cures saved Smartie's life, and also Dennie, for all her help, I couldn't have done it on my own. She said having to deal with the situation had given her back her confidence in horses, and once Guv had recovered enough, she rode him regularly while he was at her farm.

At that point in time, I didn't know what our fate would be, we could either persevere in our paradise home, and hope for future success, or give up, sell up and return to England. It all depended on what would happen in the next year or so. Our first few riding holidays had started well, I had really enjoyed leading people into the mountains on horseback...it had been my dream, and it could still come true. We had uprooted Craig, and brought him to a strange country where he didn't speak the language, yet he had settled well and was happy here, he had a good social life with many friends.

We had both been passionate about our whole adventure. We had wanted to know what it was like to live without the paraphernalia of modern life. We had stepped back in time and accomplished most things that we set out to do. But....it was hard.

Bringing water uphill from the river daily in all weathers, for all our needs. Our little spring provided our drinking water, but it still had to be collected. No electricity made for shorter days, especially in winter, and no power tools. Washing clothes by hand, which had to be wrung by hand and hung out wet. I think I missed my washing machine the most! At least we had a car; lots of our neighbours had never owned a car, they had walked everywhere for their whole lives. I was proud of myself for what I had achieved...we had all achieved.

We had done our sums, and knew that Steve would have to work in England for four months a year for the next few years, to enable us to bring our house into the 21st century. Wages here were just too low, and work was hard to find. We had been told that the ruin next to our house was for sale. It had been a little two bedroom cottage, but was now just four crumbling walls with no roof. It would make a lovely guest cottage....WOW what a project!

We had two lovely healthy foals, and I desperately wanted to be a part of their future. Also a whole family of other animals, their lives were all in our hands. We had found our paradise; I loved our house; I didn't feel that I ever wanted to leave. I had never been happier, or worked harder in my life, but could we sustain it? Only time would tell.

Our neighbour Francisco, called by with a wicker basket full of fluffy brown and yellow baby ducklings....how could I say no....but that's another story!

Printed in Great Britain
by Amazon

86852079R00123